MAKING MEN

FIVE STEPS TO GROWING UP

CHUCK HOLTON

WITH

TREVOR WILLIAMS

Published by Live Fire Books
© 2011 by Charles W. Holton
ISBN/EAN13: 0615544398 / 9780615544397

Cover image by Chuck Holton
Interior design by Janet McHenry
Author Photo by Jenna Crouch

Unless otherwise indicated, Scripture quotations are
from:
The Holy Bible, English Standard Version®
© 2011
by Crossway books

For information:
Charles Holton
www.makingmenbook.com

This book is dedicated to Ken Strunk,
who encouraged me to be a man and still does.

Contents

Prologue

"My dad didn't teach me anything about manhood, so I am winging it."

-in an email from a Christian dad.

To make a man, you must first know what one looks like.

This book presents a picture of manhood derived from my three-year study of what the Bible has to say about men. If I learned anything in that time, it's that I still have a lot to learn. I'm a passionate, driven person by nature, though, so please forgive me if I come on strong to the men reading this book. But it's not a work for men only. In fact, I believe it is vitally important for young women to study the facets of a man, because I've seen the absolutely horrific choices many women make in a life partner, whereas knowing the five facets of manhood would have saved them a lifetime of torment and regret.

Single mothers, too, often lament their sons have no positive male role model or mentor to emulate. For such women hoping to make a man out of their son, this book will provide a step-by-step guide to teaching their boy what a man looks like and what he needs to do to become one himself.

Ideally, fathers will use this book as a resource in guiding their sons into manhood. I've used it as a curriculum for my own sons and have spread its message to churches and men's groups, where I've seen it change lives around the globe. Often, married women come to me in tears after I present this study in a sermon, telling me how they wish their husbands could have been present to hear the message. I wish those husbands could see the hurt their passivity causes.

Some notes about terminology used in this book: I don't like to use terms like *godly men* or *true manhood*, because I believe qualifiers like *godly* and *true* are redundant and only dilute the meaning of the words to which they are applied. The manhood I describe in this book is certainly true and godly, but those qualities should be considered part and parcel with the words themselves. I mean, can you really have ungodly manhood?

To describe males who fail to achieve the standard of manhood, I've chosen to use the term *guys*. Such as, "*guys* collect status symbols to prove their worth, but *men* find such things unnecessary."

This work is meant to describe the most basic qualities of a man, from which all the other things we associate with "a good one" will derive. It will also explain my how I came to understand the five steps to manhood.

It's not written like a textbook, but more like a narrative about the steps that a guy must take to pick up the mantle of manhood and wear it well. Actions speak louder than words, but sometimes words can illuminate action and help make sense of it. My prayer is that in reading this work you will come to a much better understanding of what a man looks and acts like, and in so doing, you'll be motivated to make your sons men and teach your daughters to recognize them. God help us if you fail.

The world desperately needs all the men it can get.

Chapter 1
The Big Question

A Typical Saturday, Any Mall in America

Look over there, Son. See the guy with the studded leather vest and the skull-and-crossbones bandana around his head? Why do you suppose he dresses that way? And what's with the scowl on his face?

Here, sit with me. Let's watch people go by for a little while. Notice all the different looks guys choose. What about that dude—the one in the too-tight tank top coming out of the vitamin store? His arms must be the size of my thigh. Whatever supplements he's got in that bag must be working—he's got muscles on top of his muscles and tattoos covering those.

What would make a guy work that hard on his physique?

Oh, wait. Check out this kid over here. Shuffling along in saggy pants like one leg is shorter than the other. He's got his hat on sideways and a big gold chain around his neck. What kind of statement is he trying to make? What identity does he want to show the world? Does any part of that look kind of silly to you? So why does he dress that way, really?

Remember the guy we saw getting out of that seven-foot tall pickup in the parking lot? The one with flames painted on the side? Why would anyone possibly need a truck with tires that big?

It might not seem like these guys have anything in common, Son, but they do. They're all trying to answer the same question. It's a question every guy has to answer:

How will they know that I'm a man?

Don't make fun of them. One day soon you'll have to answer it, too.

The Answer

Every guy tries to find a way to answer the question, both for himself and for the world. Some respond by working hard, getting a good job, making lots of money. Others buy a crotch rocket. When I was a boy, I tried to answer that question by jumping off the roof of my house.

Fortunately not every manifestation of the answer is as stupid as that. Later on, I tried to answer the question by becoming an Airborne Ranger.

I was only seventeen when I joined the army. I joined voluntarily, but looking back I really had no choice. Oh, there was a desire to serve my country, do my duty, all that good stuff...but if I'm brutally honest, I *had* to join the military.

See, I got bullied a lot in high school. I was only a buck twenty soaking wet. Half a dozen boys in my class decided their undeclared major was to make my life miserable. As soon as I could, I joined the army and volunteered for the Rangers, because it was the best solution I could think of to make sure nobody ever picked on me again. I needed something tangible—like the Ranger beret—to prove to everyone, myself included, that I could hold my own in the land of men.

Throughout basic training, then Airborne School, and, finally, the three-week Ranger Indoctrination Program, I wanted to quit many times, but not once did I seriously entertain the thought. No way could I give up. Too much was at stake.

On graduation day I proudly donned the Ranger beret and reported for duty at the Ranger regiment, only to make a terrible discovery. I now had what I needed to prove to those high school bullies that I was a man, but they didn't matter anymore. Now I was surrounded by a tougher, meaner, been-there-done-that crowd of Rangers, who made those high-school jerks look as childish as they really were. Now I had to prove myself to a new community of tough guys, and the Ranger beret was worth little more than the price of admission.

One thought prevailed: *Here we go again.*

Looking back, I can see many of those guys were facing the same questions. How do I prove that I'm a man? What does a real man look like? How does he talk? And many of us lived by this unspoken maxim: Fake it till you make it.

Operation Just Cause

I can still hear the whirr of the C-130 aircraft engine and smell the jet fuel mixed with the fetid odor of the jungle below. I remember the jolt as my parachute deployed and the aircraft noise fading into the distance. Below the rucksack strapped to my waist, the black carpet of earth spread out, merging on the horizon with the dark curtain of night sky. The stars above mirrored the white sparks of enemy gunfire below me, as my parachute sent me hurtling the last three hundred feet to the ground. Just before impact, tracers strafed my chute. Someone was trying to kill me.

Welcome to combat.

The year was 1989. My Ranger unit parachuted into Panama on the first night of the invasion that would come to be known as Operation Just Cause. Our mission was to capture Manuel Noriega, a corrupt dictator who brutally oppressed the Panamanian people and who funded his activities with proceeds from illicit drug trade.

It was a short and violent operation. Over the Christmas holidays that year, the 75th Ranger Regiment stormed across Panama—releasing political prisoners, securing police stations and airports, and engaging in some of the most intense combat U.S. forces had faced since the Vietnam War.

Three weeks after our first drop we were sitting in a tent at Howard Air Force Base, just west of the Panama Canal, awaiting orders for our next mission. We had lost comrades in the short conflict, and we were living in that strange purgatory between longing for home and itching for the next chance to charge into battle.

When our first shipment of mail arrived, one of our guys opened a letter from his wife that included an article clipped from his hometown newspaper in Columbus, Georgia. The front-page story depicted a gallant soldier who claimed to have *Halo*-dropped into Panama prior to the invasion to clear the drop zone ahead of the Ranger assault. The story related in the article went beyond ridiculous. This soldier, one "Corporal Jefferson" reportedly spent three days chasing Noriega through the jungle, machete and M-16 in hand. According to the article, Panamanian forces had ambushed his unit, and only he had escaped to tell their tale of heroism.

The more we read, the more comical and outlandish the story became. The photo on the front page of the paper showed a young soldier sporting a tough-guy look and a bandage on his arm. But there was something wrong with his uniform—actually, a lot of somethings. The medals weren't in their proper places. It was as if a sixth grader had gone to Ranger Joe's and picked up a handful of shiny medals and stuck them on a dress uniform.

"Rangers lead the way." It's the Ranger motto. Was this joker leading the way for us? Of course, some Special Ops units were more clandestine than ours. But even if there had been a covert unit sent to mitigate resistance on the drop zone, the chance that a soldier of that caliber recounting a secret mission to a hometown newspaper remained basically nil.

No, this guy was a poser, plain and simple.

And I was going to hunt him down.

The Wannabe

As soon as we returned to Fort Benning, I donned a set of starched BDUs and grabbed my Ranger beret. It was time to take a stroll. I headed just down the block to a nearby engineer battalion. Earlier I'd made a quick call to the reporter who wrote the original story, and she told me where I could find "Corporal Jefferson." I couldn't wait to meet the man who had allegedly cleared the way for my unit and pursued one of the most infamous dictators in Latin America. If this man was half the soldier he claimed to be, and if the mission had happened as he had described, then I was about to meet a genuine hero.

Yeah, right.

I walked in and found the first sergeant.

"I'm looking for a Corporal Jefferson. Anyone here by that name?"

"No, but we have a Private Jefferson."

Hmmm...the plot thickens.

I pulled out the newspaper article and pointed at the goofy photo of the soldier wearing the misplaced medals and stripes. "Oh no!" the first sergeant gasped, then turned and bellowed down the hallway. "Get me Private Jefferson!"

A few minutes later, Jefferson walked through the door. This time, he wasn't wearing dress uniform or even fatigues. The "tough guy" from the newspaper story stood sheepishly before me in a white cook's uniform, stained from preparing the day's meal. (The bandage on his arm turned out to be a burn from mess hall duty.) His eyes widened as he took in my jump wings, combat infantryman badge, and, finally, the Ranger beret. The look of fear paralyzing his face was priceless.

"*Corporal* Jefferson!" I exclaimed, pouring on the sarcasm. "I just wanted to let you know how thankful we Rangers are that you jumped in and cleared the drop zone for us. In fact, let me shake your hand. And oh, by the way, the rest of my buddies will be over later to thank you personally as well!"

Private Jefferson collapsed into a chair and looked as though he was about to wet himself. In that moment, a wave of pity washed over me. This man, all ninety-eight or so pounds of him, had wanted everyone back home to think he was a hero. He wanted it so badly that he made up a story to prove it —all because he didn't believe he had what it takes to be a man.

The Masks of Manhood

Jefferson was a pretender, a poser. He bought a bunch of medals he hadn't earned, put them on his uniform, and went home for Christmas with stories about saving the day. Unfortunately, his facade crumbled all too soon, revealing a scared and embarrassed little boy.

When it comes to manhood, guys try to construct a mask that fits their idea of what manhood looks like. Regrettably, few have ever been shown the shape of true manhood, so the mask often ends up looking as ludicrous as Private Jefferson's make-believe dress uniform. Guys build caricatures of manhood, because they lack good role models in their lives.

All those guys at the mall exhibited little shows of what the world calls "manliness", with behaviors flashing like neon signs to convince the world they have what it takes to be a man. The grimace, muscles, staples through the eyebrows, or thousand-dollar suits—the purpose is the same. There isn't anything necessarily wrong with putting flames on your car or even on your body for that matter, but it's the *why* that sometimes makes them ridiculous. These socially reinforced masks of toughness and masculinity often turn out to be little more than Private Jefferson's medals.

Some people might say, "What's the big deal? Every guy has to craft his own identity, and for some that includes a tattoo or a fast car. So what?"

But what is identity? Is it not the picture a person shows to the world that says, "I'm a unique and worthwhile human being?" Okay, sure. But should we look to anything external to prove that? Isn't a person's uniqueness and worth endowed by his Creator? If so, does he really need a neck tattoo?

A man who knows who he is doesn't need a facade. The first thing you should notice about him is his character, an internal quality that doesn't require an ostentatious display of any kind. Believe me, true character is so rare that people will notice—even without a seven-foot-tall pickup truck.

A man knows he doesn't have to prove it.

True Character makes a man

An Example of Manhood

"Rob" is one of the manliest men I know. He's six foot two without an ounce of body fat. A member of the United States' most secretive and elite counterterrorism unit, he is probably one of the most lethal human beings you'd ever meet. This combat-hardened professional has spent most of the last ten years in combat. And when I say combat, I don't mean driving Humvees around a base or guarding a concrete block in the desert.

This man was there during the opening salvo of the war in Afghanistan. His unit dragged Saddam Hussein out of hiding and brought him to justice. He's performed hundreds of high-risk takedowns of terrorist kingpins. He's been wounded in battle. And he could probably kill you with his pinky finger.

But you'd never know any of that at first glance. Rob doesn't strut around acting like a tough guy. Doesn't need to. Good luck getting him to regale you with any been-there-done-that war stories.

Don't get me wrong. Rob *is* tough and he knows it; he just doesn't feel the need to make sure everyone else knows it, too. On the contrary, he's soft-spoken, gentle with his kids, and quick to flash a smile. He carries himself with an easy confidence that is disarming. In fact, Rob feels just as comfortable driving a Honda as he does riding a Harley. One day we talked about where this confidence came from, and I found out Rob wasn't always this way.

His decision to join the military was born out of a desire to prove that he had what it takes. "We all act out of our weakness," he told me. "All I have done, all the things I have accomplished in the military have been to get myself to the point where I was comfortable with myself as man."

My thoughts drifted to my sons as we talked, and I knew they would someday face these same questions. I don't want my boys making life-and-death decisions out of a desperate need to prove they are men. I don't want them to act out of weakness. If they become soldiers or firemen, buy a motorcycle, or get a tattoo-- whatever they decide to do—I want them to act out of an understanding of the true value of these choices. I don't want their motivation to come from desperate desires to prove their manhood to a world that really doesn't care. I don't want to raise pretenders who waste time trying to *look* strong when they could just man up and actually *be* strong.

But how? After all, I wasn't sure I had this whole manhood thing figured out myself. Even in my thirties, the question still lingered in my own life. *Am I really a man yet? When will I know I've arrived?*

I resolved to find the answers, so as to become an expert on the subject of manhood. To do that, I embarked on a several-year quest to distill the essence of manhood into a simple formula easy enough to memorize and teach to my kids.

Leave Childhood Behind

God's Word says, "When I was a child, I spoke like a child, I thought like a child, I reasoned like a child. When I became a man, I gave up childish ways" (1 Corinthians 13:11).

This first verse that my sons and I memorized reminds us how becoming a man means making the choice to leave childhood behind. It is a decision that parents should encourage their sons to make—earlier rather than later.

The second chapter of Luke shows how Jesus made this choice at the age of twelve. I've included this informative short story here and highlighted some important details.

*Now his parents went to Jerusalem every year at the Feast of the Passover. And when he was twelve years old, they went up according to custom. And when the feast was ended, as they were returning, **the boy Jesus stayed behind in Jerusalem**.*

*His parents did not know it, but supposing him to be in the group they went a day's journey, but then they began to search for him among their relatives and acquaintances, and when they did not find him, they returned to Jerusalem, searching for him. **After three days they found him in the temple, sitting among the teachers, listening to them and asking them questions.** And all who heard him were amazed at his understanding and his answers. And when his parents saw him, they were astonished. And his mother said to him, "Son, why have you treated us so? Behold, your father and I have been searching for you in great distress."*

*And he said to them, "Why were you looking for me? Did you not know that I must be in my Father's house?" And they did not understand the saying that he spoke to them. **And he went down with them and came to Nazareth and was submissive to them**. And his mother treasured up all these things in her heart.*

And Jesus increased in wisdom and in stature and in favor with God and men. — Luke 2:41-52

Let me point out a few things about this story. Jesus didn't get lost or forgotten. He chose to stay behind. He spent between three and five days, depending on how you read the time frame, in a metropolitan city all alone. In that time he presumably found food to eat and a place to stay; he then engaged himself in purposeful work, being "about his father's business."

Jesus wasn't sinning—he was beginning the work for which he came to earth. And even though his parents didn't understand his drive to serve his heavenly father, he humbled himself and was submissive to them. Because of these things, Jesus impressed both his Father in heaven and his father on earth.

Jewish boys between the age of twelve and fourteen underwent a ceremony that welcomed them into the brotherhood of men. He entered the temple, read scripture, and demonstrated knowledge about what he read.

He then was allowed to worship with the men for the first time. A twelve-year-old boy in ancient Israel was recognized as having met all the requirements of manhood.

In today's culture ask any boy or parent at what age a boy becomes a man. I'm sure you'd get lots of different answers, but I'd wager none of them would be as young as twelve.

Let Them Be Men

Boys often form an image of manhood from other boys, with few having any idea what a man really is, so it's the blind leading the blind. Worse yet, they can easily glean ideas about manhood from movies, music, and mass media, whose objective is nothing less than to sell them into slavery. To make matters worse, many boys don't have a father at home from whom to glean a positive example, which only exacerbates this troubling trend.

A boy of twelve to fourteen should have already learned the essentials of manhood from his father or from a trustworthy mentor in his father's absence. These lessons are best learned when they are demonstrated by the men around him, but just demonstrating is not enough. We don't train pilots by putting them in the cockpit of a 747 and then telling them to "watch what the pilot does." On-the-job training is effective, but only if the why and how questions are answered as well. An athlete doesn't learn to win just by watching other athletes; he must study the rules of the game in detail, then train under the watchful eye of a devoted coach.

God made fathers to be their sons' "man coach," and it is a blessed boy, indeed, whose dad is intentional about teaching him the rules of the game. This can make the difference between a son who "grows in favor with God and men," or, as they say where I live in West Virginia, one who becomes a man "of no account."

A hundred years ago, when a boy got old enough to carry water or throw hay, he was out in the fields with the other men, learning from them what men looked like, talked like, and acted like. Boys of that era looked forward to manhood.

These days, boys most often look forward to becoming teenagers, that in-between age where one has most of the faculties of an adult without any of the responsibilities. Not surprisingly, many adults do their best to act like teens, too.

"Adolescence," as it is currently understood in American culture, is a false construct. Created in the 1950s by powerful marketing firms as a way to sell things to the baby boomer generation, this view tells boys and girls that the teen years will be the best days of their lives. They're led to believe that "fun" is the end-all and be-all of their existence, and many adults are lured into this same line of thinking. Diane West put it this way in her book *The Death of the Grown-Up*:

For something like fifty years, media culture, from Hollywood to journalism to music to Madison Avenue, has increasingly idealized youth even as it
has   increasingly   lampooned   adulthood, particularly fatherhood.[i]

In his 1963 book *Teen-Age Tyranny* former New York Times education editor Fred M. Hechinger wrote:

> Instead of making adolescence a transition period, necessary and potentially even valuable (if, often slightly comical), it began to turn it into a separate way of life to be catered to, exaggerated and extended far beyond its biological duration. Eventually it became a way of life imitated by young and not-so-young adults.[ii]

In light of the great disparity between the modern and biblical models of growing up, it is important to ask ourselves where we, as concerned parents, get our concept of what true manhood looks like. We then need to strip away that which is false. Remember 2 Corinthians 10, Verse 5:

> *We destroy arguments and every lofty opinion raised against the knowledge of God, and take every thought captive to obey Christ.*

Examples Aren't Enough

I grew up in a very functional home. My dad worked hard to model godly manhood, and I did my best (except for certain painful instances) to learn from his example. But he never really sat me down and said, "Son, this is what a man does." As a result, even though he was diligent to display how a man should act, I sometimes misunderstood him and misconstrued the purposes behind what he did.

I remember one instance when we went out to eat as a family, the harried waitress forgot to bring silverware for our table. Not wanting to make a scene about it, my dad quietly slipped into the kitchen to pick up utensils for our family. But instead of getting the lesson, "A man doesn't demand to be catered to but looks for ways to make others' lives easier," my boy mind saw the sign that said "Employees Only" on the kitchen door and thought, *Wow...a man doesn't have to follow the rules.*

Silly, I know. But for a young boy, self-confidence can be easily confused with a sense of superiority. Assertiveness can look like intimidation. I knew I needed to give my sons more than my often-flawed example to go on. I wanted to point them to the perfect standard. So I went to the book that has proved itself as the source of ultimate truth time and time again—the Bible.

I went through the Bible twice and examined stories of manhood fulfilled and manhood failed. I decided to create a curriculum of sorts that would serve as a solid foundation in the essentials of manhood. I wanted to give my sons a comprehensive roadmap just in case, God forbid, I won't be here to coach them all to maturity. In short, it had to show my sons the true SHAPE of a man.

Here are the five qualities of manhood, in the form of an acronym.

Submit

Honor

Assess and Improve

Perish and Provide

Engage

But before we get into detailed discussion about each of these five facets, let me tell my story and how God taught me these principles.

Main Point
Notes from Ch. 2

Every guy tries to
figure out what man-
hood is.

A man doesn't pretend to
be something. He just is.

There is no set age
for a man to become
a man.

Submit

Honor

Assess + Improve

Perish + Provide

Engage

Chapter 2
My Story

I had landed the kind of career most guys would kill for, starting with the great pay and generous benefits. I set my own hours, and the exciting work challenged me. The job? A stockbroker for a reputable firm in Washington, D.C.

One of my favorite aspects of being a broker was doing research—sifting through reams of data and looking for trends to help my clients make money. I'd been working at the job for almost eight years when I noticed a trend of a different sort, one that would have a profound effect on my life.

Most of my clients were wealthy middle-aged men. Multi-millionaires, some of them. Over the years I had gotten to know them during phone conversations as we discussed their portfolios. At some point, all of them expressed to me the same abiding regret: "I just wish I had spent more time with my kids."

At the time, I liked to tell people my life was a SITCOM: Single Income, Three Children, Oppressive Mortgage. For all the excitement and profit it held, my job consumed me. I left the house when my little ones were getting up in the morning and came home about an hour before their bedtime. My weekends consisted of trying to keep our farm from falling down around us and participating in church activities. To my kids, Daddy was just a guy who slept at their house and worked long hours staring at a computer. In short, I was traveling on the same road as my clients—the road to wealth…and regrets.

But I've always wanted to be the kind of guy who could learn from others' mistakes. I didn't want to look back on my life with remorse for not building a strong family legacy. I wanted my kids to know they were more important to me than that computer I pecked away at ten hours a day.

But how? The bills had to get paid. Apart from becoming independently wealthy, I still had to find a way to make ends meet. So I started planning…and praying. My prayer went something like this. "Lord, please help me find a way to restructure my life, so that I can spend more time with my family and still honor my responsibility to provide for them."

The solution grew slowly, like a carefully constructed building from blueprints full of ideas. Looking back, I see now that it was a process of maturing and learning more about what it truly means to be "the man of the house."

I was making a living teaching people how to preserve their assets, diversify their investments, and leverage their financial resources to be more profitable. At some point it occurred to me how those same ideas could be effective in other areas of my life.

- What if I worked to preserve the one asset I can never get more of—time?

- What if I tried to diversify not only my investments but also my whole life?

- What if I applied the concept of leverage to my time?

Probing those "what ifs" led me first to look for more sources of income, since it was the most concrete of the three. I determined that I didn't need more money, but I did need more freedom. The problem with having only one source of income was that I was owned by that one source. I couldn't live without it, so I was a slave to the requirements of the job, no matter how much it kept me from more important things. More time with the kids meant less time at the office. That would require a broader financial horizon to keep me from being too dependent on my day job. Finding another source of income that paid as much as my brokerage job would be a real challenge, but that wasn't my goal.

Instead, I wanted a collection of small income streams, preferably ones that didn't require a large up-front investment or an ongoing commitment of my time.   Every additional source of income made it a little easier to knock off early at the brokerage firm and spend some time with the kids. It turned out to be easier than I expected. I discovered there are lots of ways to make, say, a hundred dollars a month that many people pass up because it's not enough to live on. But, with a little creativity, we were able to diversify our cash flow in small ways. And once I learned to see the opportunities, I found them almost everywhere.

I'm telling this part of my story because it is a dilemma that nearly every man faces at some point in his life. He's duty-bound to provide for his family, but in so doing, he often feels forced to neglect that very family. Most careers today afford no slack and consume all of a man's time and attention, if given the chance. A man's vocation also offers meaning and purpose, leading a man to look to his work for needed affirmation. In those two ways, a man's work can possess great power over him. My sons will face this dilemma, too. I had to find a way to conquer it so I could teach them to do the same.

I figured diversifying my cash flow would diminish each income stream's ability to consume me. I'd be less apt to worry about losing one source of income if nine more were still contributing to the pot. In that way each income stream would hold limited sway over my family.

Second, developing ten sources of income would, by necessity, require several to be passive or semi-passive in nature. I couldn't work ten part-time jobs, even if I wanted to; some would have to run on their own. I wasn't sure how to accomplish that goal when I started, but I began with one maxim: Make everything profitable. I committed myself not to waste time, energy, or resources.

As a commissioned employee of the brokerage firm, I was essentially unemployed every day until I went out and found something to sell. Not a bad way to make a living, since there was plenty of money to be managed. But that fact only contributed to the feeling that I needed to work as hard as possible all the time—because the job never got "finished," and because the market could dry up tomorrow. The core issue came down to self-discipline but not in the way I had been trained to apply it.

The military taught me that you don't quit until the mission is accomplished. When I became a broker, I brought that attitude to the office. My mission was to make money for my clients. But how much is enough? No matter how long or how hard I worked, the thought pursued me that I could make just a little more. After almost a decade of running hard, I finally decided I had entered the wrong race.

It was time to redefine my mission.

I started looking for new sources of income, with the goal of reducing my time at the office. The idea of writing interested me, as I could do it late at night after everyone was asleep. Besides the initial potential of a few extra dollars, everything I wrote could be sold many times over to different markets. That was the kind of income I had in mind.

My wife and I also looked at a number of ways to make our farm profitable. First, we purchased a few pigs to fatten for market (not necessarily a venture I recommend, especially if you live in a condo). I researched other ideas to glean how we could put part of our land into a government easement program that paid us to grow trees. I started a discussion forum for small farmers online (www.homesteadingtoday.com) and began to collect advertising revenue. We finished off the space above our garage and rented it to a newlywed couple. Within a couple years, we diversified our income into a half-dozen sources.

Unfortunately, making more money didn't solve the problem. I still wasn't spending more time at home. If anything, I was working harder than ever as the stock market entered a protracted bear cycle.

When my writing career started to pick up steam, I sensed that God was calling me to quit my job as a broker, give up all my security and benefits, and become a full-time writer. The idea stopped just short of ludicrous.

Almost no one, especially in the Christian market, writes full time for a living. All the writers I'd met at conferences said the same thing: writing is something you do on the side. I agreed with their conclusion—after all, a freelance writer doesn't get health insurance, stock options, or a 401K. He might get paid only once every six months. Still, I couldn't shake the feeling deep down in my spirit that was telling me to step out in faith and leave the financial services business behind.

I wrestled with these feelings for some time. Then, one weekend at a Christian booksellers' convention in Florida, I had the chance to spend some time with one of my writing heroes, Randy Alcorn.

Randy's life reads like a study in living one's priorities. After helping found the Good Shepherd Community Church outside of Portland and serving as a pastor for fourteen years, Randy took part in a number of nonviolent pro-life events in front of abortion clinics. Due to his involvement, he washauled into court by two clinicsm the second of which levied a judgment against him and others for an astounding eight million dollars.

After his first judgment they came to garnish his wages from his church, and because he couldn't justify paying even a dime to an abortion clinic, Randy resigned and began writing full time.

In retrospect, God's guiding hand is more than obvious. Today Randy is a best-selling author whose books have touched countless lives around the world. And despite the millions of books he's sold, the abortion clinic has never received a cent of his paycheck, because Randy pays himself only minimum wage, giving all of the his writing royalties to charity.

I cornered him on a bus as we headed to dinner one evening at the convention.

"Could I ask you a question, Randy?"

"Sure."

"Well, I've been feeling for a while now that God is calling me to write full time. But everyone says it's hard to make a living as a writer."

"That's true."

"Well, how do I resolve this compulsion to write with my responsibility to provide for my family?"

Randy thought for a moment. "Who told you it was your responsibility to provide for your family?"

His question delivered instant confusion. "What do you mean? I've always been taught that a man who doesn't provide for the members of his household is worse than an unbeliever. Doesn't the Bible say that?"

Randy nodded. "Yes, but it also tells us in Matthew 6 not to worry about what we will eat or what we will wear, but to seek first his kingdom and righteousness, and 'all these things will be added unto you.'"

Randy's words punched me in the gut.

"It comes down to this," he said. "Your 'job' is to be obedient, not to make money. If you will follow God's leading, you will never have to worry about God's provision. Don't fall victim to thinking that you are the one doing the providing."

My new mission had finally crystallized.

Later that night in my hotel room, I got on my knees next to the bed. It was time for a serious discussion with my Maker.

"Father," I began, "I want to be obedient to your will. But I need to know for sure that I'm hearing you correctly. I'm willing to leave the security of my job at the brokerage firm if that's what you want me to do. But I need to know that I'm not feeling this way because I'm burned out as a broker, or because some part of me wants to be a famous author, or for any other reason. My heart is deceitful and wicked, so please help me separate what my heart is telling me from what you are telling me. Make it clear, and I will do whatever you call me to do."

In short, I resubmitted my life to God, signed a blank check, and handed it over to him. A sense of peace descended on the heels of that decision. After all, I reasoned in my quirky way, if everything went south now, well, I could blame it on God.

I'm actually not sure why that made me feel better....

I had been writing a series of articles for Focus on the Family's teen magazine *Breakaway* about positive male role models. The week after the convention, I heard about a seventy-year-old man who had literally run across America passing out Bibles from coast to coast. I decided he'd make a good story for the series and called him at his home in Phoenix.

"I'm a freelance writer," I explained, introducing myself over the phone. "I'm writing a series of stories about positive male role models, and I think your story would be a good fit. Would you be willing to grant an interview?"

"Sure, I would."

"Great. I'm going backpacking for the next week, but when I return, I'll call you and have you tell me your story. Let me leave you my phone number in case you need to reach me in the meantime."

"Sounds good. Talk to you next week."

A week later I returned to civilization and found a curious message in my voicemail from the man in Phoenix. "Mr. Holton, please call. It's urgent."

Wondering what could be urgent from a guy I barely knew, I dialed his number.

He sounded uncomfortable when I identified myself on the phone. "Mr. Holton, I hope what I'm going to say won't offend you. I never do things like this, but I just feel very strongly that I'm supposed to give you a message."

Okay…that's not something you hear every day. "What's the message?"

He hesitated. "Well, you have to understand that I spent forty years in business and was very successful. I made millions of dollars."

"Yes…but what does that have to do with me?"

The man began to cry, and I couldn't imagine what he was going to say next. "It's just that I would give up every dollar right now if I could spend one more hour with my son, who just died of cancer at age thirty-nine."

He continued, sobbing now. "I don't know why, Mr. Holton, but I just feel like I'm supposed to tell you not to make that mistake."

Boom…there it was. God's answer to my prayer. And he had made it *very* clear.

Chapter 3
Submit

As a teen, I wanted to prove my manhood, so I joined the Marine Corps. But shortly before I was commissioned as an officer, a back injury ended that career before it started. Feeling empty and still unproven, I turned to a business career and did whatever it took to achieve. Fifteen years passed and though I did extremely well, I still felt emptier than ever. By that time, I had begun to believe that I would always be found lacking, that my wife would never be pleased and that my children would be disappointed in me. So, like my father, I gave up. I made a series of increasingly bad decisions that should have cost me everything.

At my very bottom, I distinctly remember asking myself, "Do you really even believe there is a God?" It was sobering. I was dead serious. Finally I made up my mind, "Yes, I do."

That is when I gave up for the second time. This time, I gave up control of everything to Him. That was the moment when I began to stop feeling like I had to measure up.

--Mike in Ohio

It's every man's secret—insecurity. It frames the questions he asks himself in the dark when nobody else is around. *Have I made it yet? Do I make the cut? How do I prove that I'm a man?* These questions haunt even those who appear successful, fit, and confident —with good jobs, homes, and families.

Many guys look for the answer to those questions for their entire lives and never find it. But it's not for a lack of trying. Take a look around at the behaviors our society views as "masculine," and ask yourself if they aren't better explained as the actions of overgrown boys desperately seeking affirmation.

Fortunately, becoming a man doesn't require a college degree or being muscular or pierced like a fish. Unfortunately, what it does require is much more difficult. It all starts with surrender.

The Gateway to Manhood

Many guys believe authentic manhood means finding ways to prove they don't need anybody—like a rugged cowboy going it alone.

But if I was indeed *created* to be a man, then the first necessary step to claiming that quality is submission. I must give myself wholeheartedly to the purpose for which I was created. This simply requires placing my life back into the capable hands of my Creator. To fulfill my destiny, I can only do so by trusting the One who put me here in the first place.

Submission, then, is the gateway to manhood, and many guys miss it. They spend their whole lives fiercely trying to prove their independence. This rebellion robs them of the great authority they're entitled to as men. We'll talk more about that authority later.

Consider a stallion roaming wild, a majestic creature, full of strength and beauty. With thundering hooves and rippling muscles, he is a formidable force of nature. But if he never submits to the bit and bridle, he will never be useful; his untamed strength will be a liability, not an asset to the world around him.

For many, submission seems like a step in the wrong direction. Men are supposed to be in control—masters of their domain and destiny. But think about it for a minute. Life is full of paradoxes like this. My drill sergeant put it this way: You can't lead until you know how to follow.

Basic Combat Training

When I joined the army, I was ready for what I thought would be a wild first experience: basic *combat* training. A skinny kid at the time, I fancied myself emerging after months of boot camp as a lean, mean fighting machine, torching buildings with flamethrowers and rappelling from helicopters. I envisioned myself as an intimidating and dangerous "Army of One" and that everyone would then *know* I was a man.

But after the first few weeks of boot camp, I wanted a refund. We weren't being taught martial arts, and I daresay there wasn't a flamethrower anywhere on base. Instead, we were being taught how to walk right, talk right, eat right, sit right — all things I was pretty sure I already knew how to do. We spent hours shining our boots, making our beds, and folding our underwear into six-by-six-inch squares.

In my mind this "training" had nothing to do with combat. Where were the guns and the explosives, the ninja stars and the throwing knives? Instead of learning how to kill people with our bare hands, we were being made to relearn everything "the army way." I didn't feel lean and mean. I felt cheated.

My frustration grew with my every thought. *This is a classic bait and switch. What's the purpose of all this? What do barracks inspections and standing at attention have to do with being a warrior?*

As we continued the course, I found myself increasingly disillusioned. I began to despise my drill sergeant named Febus. His sole purpose, I decided, was to make us miserable in every way, while we blindly followed instructions that had little to do with fighting.

But as the training continued, my thoughts shifted. My drill sergeant had been on the battlefield and knew what it took to stay alive in combat. He had a vested interest in making sure we were the best soldiers we could be. As time went on, our platoon was transformed from a gaggle of inexperienced civilians into a cohesive unit of soldiers. The process of all those shared ordeals—waxing the barracks floor in the middle of the night, enduring long ruck marches, and doing PT in the mud—shaped us into a team that functioned almost as one body. Drill Sergeant Febus was using all those miserable experiences to build disciplined warriors one small brick at a time. By the time graduation rolled around, I knew I could count on the soldiers around me, because I had seen them endure.

I could have regained "independence" by quitting, but by submitting to my drill sergeant, even when his commands made no sense, I learned to work as a part of a team. In so doing, I became a part of something bigger than myself.

God created every boy on purpose. That purpose is all part of his great plan for this world. Submitted to God, a man will find a new kind of freedom and power to be more than he could ever be on his own.

Picture the knight of the medieval era. Singled out as a young boy, he was sent off to the castle to become a page and be trained in the arts of knighthood. His entire life was devoted to becoming a knight. He trained to fight, to hunt, to ride a horse—and also to serve. He learned the code of chivalry. Up to fifteen years of intensive training were required to accrue the skills needed to join the order. By the time his training was completed, he was strong and proficient in battle. He knew what honor looked like.

But before he could join the ranks of "servant soldiers," one final step awaited. During a ceremony, or "accolade," the knight-elect would kneel or bow before the monarch in a symbolic gesture of submission—not just to the king, but also to the tenets of the order. The knight was signifying his willingness to fulfill the duties that came with the job.

Have you ever wondered why we bow our heads when we pray? It comes from that same tradition. Submission is the gateway, the first step on the road to manhood.

The Father-Son Talk

My oldest boy Mason sat across from me in my office. A gangly eleven-year-old yet to grow out of the desire to be like his dad, he was leaning forward to listen as I began our first session.

"Son," I began, "God has given me the job of coaching you into manhood. No athlete becomes a champion without a coach, and I'm here to train you in the art of being a man. Now, part of a coach's job is to push you to go further than you could go alone—to make you do what is necessary to win. But you won't always like it. That's okay. A coach isn't supposed to help you feel good; he is supposed to help you *be* good."

Mason nodded. "Yes, Sir."

"So whenever you get discouraged, remember this. God created you for manhood, and he put me here to show you the way. I want nothing more than to see you succeed in becoming a godly man. The world needs all the good men it can get, son. I'm going to train you to be one of them. But before we can start the process, you need to be with me one hundred percent. Are you willing to submit to me and be trained as a man?"

His Adam's apple bobbed as he swallowed hard and nodded. I was pleased he was taking this seriously. Inside I smiled. *He is ready.*

Submission holds a negative connotation in today's world, but think of it this way: the light bulb stays in the dark until it submits to the power grid. God possesses the power to accomplish his purpose in you, but first you have to plug into his plan.

To do anything worthwhile, a guy must realize he can't do everything. He must acknowledge his need of a Commander. He must learn to obey orders. To be courageous, he must first fear the right things.

You will not find a man in the Bible who became great without first acknowledging his subservience to God. The principle of humbling oneself to be exalted is ubiquitous throughout scripture. Submitting to God's will isn't always easy, but it is *always* worth it.

There are all kinds of tough guys running around out there: sports figures, business magnates, movie stars—even military heroes. But, listen to me: regardless of how tough, rich, successful, strong, or heroic they might appear, if they have not submitted themselves to God, they are not true men, and you should not emulate them.

Don't forget: surrender is the first step to victory.

The Father-Son Relationship

Boys and their fathers must go through a difficult time when their relationship undergoes a major overhaul. A boy's relationship with his father starts out kind of like the private and the drill sergeant—one is the subordinate and the other is the superior. When Dad says "Jump," the son jumps. At some point, though, the father-son relationship must mature into a peer-to-peer relationship, with mutual respect between equal men. Having now been on both sides of this transition, I can say with certainty it isn't easy for either party. It's not that both don't want it to happen; it's just that disagreement often precipitates the timing of the shift.

When I was fifteen, I was ready to take over the world. My dad was doubtlessly thinking, "Hold on there, Big Fella. You were in diapers, what, the day before yesterday?"

Now it's my turn. I watch my teenager driving my Ford F-250 around our farm and wonder how he can reach the pedals. Because, after all, it seems he was only two feet tall the day before yesterday.

Think time flies when you are having fun? Try having kids.

Some parents refuse to treat their sons like adults, no matter what their age. Pray you won't be that way when your turn comes.

But even if that is the case with your father, a man does what's right in a relationship even if the other party hadn't or won't play along. Your duty to submit to God and the authorities he places over you isn't contingent on anyone else's performance. Your dad wasn't perfect when you were growing up? So what? Man up and do your part by showing him respect as your father. If you are a teenager, you have only a few short years left before you can get out on your own. The grace, or lack of it, that you display now with your parents will set the tone for that relationship for the rest of your life. Don't wreck it just because you can't be patient. Bide your time. Before long you'll find yourself in your parents' shoes, wondering how your son grew up so fast.

What Submission Looks Like

So, if submission is the gateway to manhood, how does one enter in?

Start with the book of Proverbs. Proverbs is a collection of wise sayings, warnings, and teachings— all penned from a father to his son. Submission is interwoven into the fabric of the entire book, starting with Chapter 1, verse 5:

A wise man will listen and increase his learning, and a discerning man will obtain guidance.[iii]

Both of these actions, listening and obtaining guidance, denote submission. But this kind of submission isn't passive. These verbs show an active pursuit of wisdom.

In short, *you've got to want it.*

Now look at verse 7:

The fear of the LORD is the beginning of knowledge; fools despise wisdom and instruction.

My study Bible points out in the footnotes, "The 'fear of the Lord' involves worship of the Lord and respectful submission to his authority in every area of life."

The world will tell you to make truth up as you go along. But a man needs an immovable foundation upon which to build his life. Let the Bible be your standard of Truth.

Be a man of action. The Proverbs are rife with words that connote action: search, seek, call out, guard. You get the picture. Now check out Chapter 1, verse 23:

If you turn to my discipline, then I will pour out my spirit on you and teach you my words.[iv]

Do you need help in figuring out this whole manhood thing? Me, too. Here's the promise in scripture—timeless words penned for guys like me.

Submit to God's ways and his Holy Spirit becomes your man coach. For life. Gentlemen, it doesn't get any better than this: a solid foundation upon which to build your life and an ever-present architect to guide you in its construction.

The Job of a Coach

I played soccer throughout junior high and high school. Most of the time, I was convinced that my coach was an absolute sadist. He just loved to make us run sprints, do passing drills, run more sprints, perform pushups, and, occasionally, go on a long distance run. Funny, I thought we were there to play soccer.

But Coach wouldn't let us scrimmage until we'd worked on the finer points of passing, dribbling, and shooting, and, as I mentioned, a few dozen wind sprints.

But he must have done something right, because we routinely crushed our competitors in the final half of the game. When the other teams got tired, we got busy and beat them. My freshman year we took first in the state for our division.

Our coach was good, because he understood that it was his job to make us *be* good, not *feel* good. At every practice, he pushed us further than we would have gone on our own, further than we believed we were capable of going.

Most of the time I hated him because he caused me so much pain. My immaturity prevented me from understanding what he was trying to do—make me a winner.

God often puts people in our lives to make us better. Those authority figures often rub us the wrong way, because they make us do the things we don't want to do. But that is the function of a good coach.

The Man-Coach

In ancient Sparta, boys were trained from child-hood to become soldiers. Stephen Pressfield describes their training in his book *The Warrior Ethos*.

> When they were boys, Alexander and his friends were forced to bathe in frigid rivers, run barefoot till their soles grew as thick as leather, ride all day without food or water and endure whippings and ritual humiliations. On the rare occasions when they got to rest, their trainers would remind them, "While you lie here at ease, the sons of the Persians are training to defeat you in battle."[v]

The Persians aren't much of a threat anymore. But they've been replaced by the very culture in which we live. Unfortunately, some parents think sons are like pets, to be pampered and fed a steady diet of leisure.

Nothing could be further from the truth. Boyhood is the time when challenges should be introduced under the watchful eye of his coach for the express purpose of hardening him to the realities of life. "Fun" should be secondary to developing a robust character, a keen sense of right and wrong, and toughness for the battles ahead. Douglas Wilson puts it this way:

> Men who follow Jesus Christ, the dragon slayer, must themselves become lesser dragon-slayers. And this is why it is absolutely essential for boys to play with wooden swords and plastic guns. Boys must learn that they are growing up to fight in a great war, and they must consequently learn, as boys, to be strong, sacrificial, courageous and good.[vi]

How does a boy learn to be strong? By carrying heavy loads. Sacrificial? By going without things he'd like to have. Courageous? By facing uncertainty. And good? By being exposed to the effects of evil.

As their father, I am the man coach for my three sons. Some boys' coach might be a relative, or out of necessity, even their mother. Anyone who cares can do the job, but whoever assumes the role, a good coach understands that **the constructive application of misery in boys' lives produces character.**

Because I remember all too well the hours of stacking wood, pulling weeds, and raking leaves I was subjected to as a boy, I won't be surprised when my three young men resent me a little when I introduce hardship into their lives. But that's okay. I'm sure someday they'll understand. Coaches, let's not grow weary in the struggle and give in to our boys when they want to take it easy. One of the best ways to keep a teen out of trouble is to ensure he's too tired from the day's work to go looking for it.

Too many parents make the mistake of thinking their job is to shelter their children from all discomfort, difficulty, and risk. But that's not what a coach does. A coach is the combination of a compass and cattle prod, to point the way and then get 'em moving. Comfort doesn't even enter into the equation.

Of this I am sure: to the extent that I can train my boys to endure and even embrace hardship, their lives will be better for it in the long run.

If you are a man-in-training, it helps if you can understand why the coach makes you miserable. It's not because he hates you--quite the contrary. If he hated you, he wouldn't bother trying to make you better. I have to remember this truth, even in my forties, because the Holy Spirit continues the work of making me more like Jesus, often through the constructive application of misery in my life.

Maybe for one reason or another your dad didn't, can't, or won't take on the role of coach. Well, never fear. Plenty of good men are out there who will happily assume that role when you convince them you sincerely value their opinion. Failing that, go back and read Proverbs again. There's a lifetime of coaching in those pages, and the Holy Spirit will illuminate their truths.

Fearing the Commander

Submission isn't a one-time deal. Every day we have to submit ourselves to the process of becoming a better soldier in God's army. That means unwavering obedience to the Commander, no matter what he asks us to give up or take up.

The Apostle Paul knew about this type of submission. In his former career as Saul, he fought against the early church to the point when he gave his approval to those who murdered believers. But then he learned to fear God through a blinding light on the road to Damascus, when he submitted to his Creator and became one of history's greatest evangelists to spread the Christian message in the first century. To get to that point, though, Paul had to accept one of the most daunting calls to ministry any man has ever heard. "Come," Jesus said, "let me show you how much you must suffer for my name" (Acts 9:16, paraphrased).

Uh…sign me up, right?

Later, beaten and imprisoned, Paul wrote to young Timothy, his apprentice. Paul shared with Timothy the secret to being effective as a man and as a believer: Don't shun suffering; embrace it:

Share in suffering as a good soldier of Christ Jesus. No soldier gets entangled in civilian pursuits, since his aim is to please the one who enlisted him.

—2 Timothy 2:3-4

Paul suffered much during his years of ministry, but he didn't follow Christ looking for a good time. Instead, he obtained something much more valuable: purpose. He wanted a life that meant something.

Which one will you choose?

A Note to Teenage Boys

Many teenage boys miss this crucial principle of submission while growing up and then often inflict permanent damage to their most important relationships. By age sixteen a boy is usually chafing to be out on his own, because our society artificially extends childhood much longer than necessary. But, ready or not, a teenager still lives at home--in Dad's house, by Dad's rules. Sometimes it's too much to take, and the father/son relationship starts to resemble a pro-wrestling grudge match. Not good.

Relationships take effort. They only flourish when both parties work to keep the bond strong. Okay, so if you're seventeen, you probably think your dad is an idiot. I did. (Somehow my dad is a lot smarter now!) Perhaps you would give anything just to have a dad who cares. Either way, the only part of the equation you can control is what *you* bring to the table. Is it worth it for you to follow your father's lead—to accept his leadership for the few short months or years you have left at home?

Think of it this way. He'll never *stop* being your dad. If you ruin the relationship now through stiff-necked rebellion, how long will you pay the price? And it won't just affect the rest of your life.

Destroying the father-son relationship will likely affect your children and the rest of your family forever. But if you can be a man and stay civilized for the next couple of years, after that you can leave home and do
things your way. Chances are, you'll still have a friend and confidant in your father. Remember the story of Jesus at age twelve? His parents didn't understand his capabilities either, but Jesus submitted himself to them anyway. You will be wise to follow his example.

Chapter 4
Honor

Remember the man I'd just met over the phone who warned me not to miss out on time with my kids? There was no denying that his call was the confirmation I had been looking for. A few days after that timely phone call, I walked into my partner's office at the brokerage firm. We shared the same name, and Chuck had always been more than just a co-worker. I had met him while serving with his son in the Army, and he had given me my big break in the business. A driven man, Chuck was also gentle and generous. We worked side-by-side managing our portfolio for nearly ten years. Besides being my mentor, he had become one of my closest friends. This promised to be one of the most difficult conversations of my life.

"Chuck," I began, "I...I've got to go."

"Go?" he questioned, still staring at his computer. "Go where?"

"I'm leaving the firm."

"What?" He swiveled to face me. "Why?"

I proceeded to explain the whole story—wanting to spend more time with my kids, planning to diversify my cash flow, and feeling called to write full time.

Always a great listener, Chuck heard me out with a furrowed brow. He had made it no secret over the years how he had high expectations for me in the brokerage business. I knew he didn't want to see me throw my career away.

He leaned forward. "Listen, I hear what you are saying. In fact, I have the same regret—wishing I had spent more time with my children. But I just want to be sure you fully understand what you are proposing. What kind of income can you make writing?"

I shrugged. "I don't know for sure. Not as much as I make here."

"What about health insurance?"

"None. I'll try to pick up an inexpensive policy to protect us in case of a catastrophe."

I could tell Chuck didn't like my answers. He looked at me for a moment, obviously trying to think of a way to get through to me. "Listen," he said finally. "I know how much you like to travel. You know you won't be able to afford that any longer."

He was right. Travel was my passion. I had been spoiling Connie and myself for the last few years, jetting off to the West Indies for an annual week of scuba diving.

The sapphire water and sandy shores would now most likely be only a distant memory. I nodded. "You're right, Chuck. But if that's the price I have to pay for not having regrets, I'm willing to give it up. In reality, I'd rather live like a pauper for the next twenty years than go to my grave wishing I had spent more time at home."

Chuck sat back in his chair and nodded. "Well then, you have my blessing. We will miss you here, but I understand what you have to do."

His answer meant more to me than he would ever know.

Now here's the funny part of the story. In the twelve months after I left the corporate world, I often traveled for speaking engagements and other opportunities God brought my way. In fact, these days I visit more than a dozen countries each year. I can't imagine going back to the confines of my office at the brokerage firm. And though I might not make as much money as I used to, our finances are much more solid than they were back then. Not because of my great business sense—far from it. In fact, I'm not sure how financial stability happened, but I do know that answering God's call was the best decision I ever made.

A missionary once told me, "God calls us to take up our cross and follow him. But when we get there, we find we gave up nothing at all." That's exactly what I found when I stepped out on faith.

It's as though God was saying, "I have so much more waiting for you! If you'll just listen and obey, you'll be more fulfilled than you ever thought possible, because you'll be doing exactly what I have called you to do."

The Definition of Honor

The subject of honor comes up in gladiator movies and Old Testament dialogues, but rarely in today's conversations. Why is that? Most guys want to be honorable, but if you'd ask a hundred men to define the word, you'd be more likely to get a laundry list of positive words like *respect, courage*, and *reverence*. Most men can describe honor, but they have a hard time nailing it down with a solid and complete definition.

If you are hunting something, it's important to know what your quarry looks like. That's why we need to form a comprehensive definition of the word *honor*. A man's sense of honor affects his life and his legacy. Important stuff.

We know honor is good and desirable and would probably equate it with qualities like virtue and respect, responsibility and propriety, or, in other words, doing the right thing.

Everyone would most likely agree that it emanates from a man's true character and would associate it with courage and obligation. All of these are true, but let's come up with a simpler definition—one we can teach to each other and to our sons.

So here's my simple definition of *honor*: "the quality of valuing things rightly; the practice of giving everything its proper place, based on a valid assessment of what it is worth."

If I have a rock in one hand and my iPhone in the other, and I have to choose between the two, I'll choose my iPhone. That's because I understand its value. The rock can't help me find the nearest Mexican restaurant. It can't remind me what I was supposed to get at the grocery store. It can't record photos of my kids. Plus, the rock didn't cost me three hundred bucks. Bye-bye, rock.

But if I'm suddenly forced to choose between my iPhone and my best friend, well, the iPhone loses. People are more important than things. An honorable man knows that.

But what if I then have to make a choice between my friend and my wife? Sorry, Buddy, but you've got to go. My wife is more important than even my own life.

You get the picture. Every choice is a value judgment. And every choice comes with a cost--in time, energy, and resources. The honorable life is one spent on things that matter.

Understanding honor requires nothing more than learning what is most important and living appropriately based on that knowledge. To honor something means to put it in its proper place, to ascribe to it the appropriate respect. Honoring God takes us back to the first principle of manhood—submitting to his sovereign will.

In order to teach the concept of value, Jesus often used money to illustrate spiritual truths. He compared God's kingdom to a treasure in a field. When a man found a smooth and shiny pearl, he instantly knew it was different from the dry soil and jagged stones that had covered it. He sold everything he had and bought the whole field. The pearl had value, and he reoriented his entire existence based on what he had found.

The honorable man follows that example. He weighs his choices carefully. In today's world he's more likely to be weighing abstract commodities like time, indulgences, and devotion, rather than jewels. Even dealing in those more nebulous currencies, the honorable man distinguishes between treasure and trash, and he pursues and protects those things that are most valuable.

Almost more importantly, a man must be hardnosed in identifying that which is worthless. He must then reject those worthless things with a passion, born of an understanding of just how finite and precious life is.

Teaching my sons about manhood means helping them understand precepts like:

- Your siblings are more important than your stuff.
- A peaceful home is more important than getting everything you want.
- Even though it might seem you have all the time in the world, your life will be gone before you know it.
- Take every thought captive, and make every action profitable.
- Look at things through the lens of eternity.
- Doing a good job is more important than getting credit.
- Loving is more important than getting what is fair.
- Your values are more important than anything.

Notice the common denominator. It's not that *you* aren't important, but a man must have security and confidence to make the tough decisions that put others ahead of himself.

One Man's Treasure...

Billy Jean James, 67, had been missing for months. Several organized searches in the desert near her home in Las Vegas, Nevada, had failed to turn up any sign of her. When they found her, it was too late. Billy Jean was dead. What baffled everyone was the fact that she was found inside her own home. Billy Jean was a hoarder. She suffered from a mental condition that made her feel the need to keep everything. She just couldn't throw anything away. Police had searched her home several times but claimed there was so much garbage throughout the dwelling they had been unable to find her body— apparently buried beneath a pile of trash.

Billy Jean's disease rendered her unable to differentiate between something valuable and something worthless. So, she kept everything—junk mail, kitchen garbage, even used cat litter. People affected by this condition have a hampered ability to determine value, and, as a result, their homes become landfills, totally unfit for human habitation. Trash shares space with furniture, and worthless trinkets become treasures. The kids get asthma, and mounds of debris become breeding grounds for bacteria. The rising piles stoke tensions, as the families struggle to understand why their loved ones value garage-sale garbage over healthy relationships.

The Treasure of Time

Hoarding, in the extreme sense, affects a small percentage of the population. But many guys suffer from a related condition—one that makes them unable to prioritize their time. They struggle to put the most important things at the top of the heap and get rid of time-wasting activities that have no redeeming value. In fact, I'd say most men battle this tendency from time to time.

Schedules are often jammed with events, meetings, and appointments designed to make guys feel important. But those same guys often end up living in

a small corner of God's plan for their lives, neglecting faith, family, and fitness, because they just "don't have any time" for them.

Conversations like this one are all too common:

Bob: "Hey John. How's it going?"

John: "Oh, man, I'm busier than a one-armed wallpaper hanger. Logged seventy-six hours last week!"

Bob: "I know what you mean. I've been traveling so much lately my kids think I died."

John: "Well, what are you going to do? Gotta put food on the table!"

Bob: "Yep. Beats being broke!"

All true. A family has to eat. A man shouldn't just lie around. The conversation takes on an air of mock regret, but underneath are thinly veiled pleas for approval. Guys want to hear an "Attaboy!" for working themselves to death. Is it honorable, though? Is it really valuing the most valuable things? Is being a slave to your job, chained to your oars seventy hours a week, really something to brag about?

God never gives any man too much to do. A man who allows himself to get over-committed at work is, in a way, sending God a message:

There must be some mistake here, God. Only twenty-four hours in a day? Are you kidding? Either you gave me too much to accomplish, or you didn't give me enough time to do it.

But it's not that there isn't enough time; it's just that we waste so much of it.

The stoic philosopher Seneca put it this way:

It is not that we have so little time but that we lose so much. Life is long enough and our allotted portion generous enough for our most ambitious projects if we invest it all carefully. But when it is squandered through luxury and indifference, and spent for no good end, we realize it has gone, under the pressure of the ultimate necessity, before we were aware it was going. So it is: **the life we receive is not short but we make it so**; we are not ill provided but use what we have wastefully.[vii]

The man whose life is one big "too busy" has allowed outside forces to dictate the course of his life, rather than structuring it in such a way as to earn the best return on his investment for God. The too-busy man is not proving his worth; he's proving that he is inefficient.

Here's the good news: inefficiency can be fixed.

I've found that about eighty percent of the stuff I spend time on every day amounts to little more than minutiae—stuff that won't matter one bit in a year, much less eternity. Being an honorable man means making a sustained and valiant effort to weed out the clutter and nurture the most important things. I have to strive to be more than careful with my time. I must be militant with myself to wring every drop of usefulness out of the vapor that is my life. But I've found that does not mean I have to keep my nose to the grindstone eighteen hours a day. Thank God.

There was a time when I believed I had to work seventy-hour weeks or my family and I would simply go broke and have to live on the street. This hard lesson took a long time to learn: living on the street with my priorities straight would be better than living in a beachfront mansion while spending my life on all the wrong things. My seventy-hour-a-week mindset stemmed more from a lack of faith—my belief that it was all up to me—as if God didn't have my life under control.

You are twenty-four hours closer to death today than you were yesterday. Time is our most valuable resource, period. It is scarce, and it is universally diminishing at every moment for every person. Being a man of honor requires that we consider the time cost of every choice.

A man will not play games with the people who matter most. He will not try to convince himself that he'll do the right thing later, as soon as the present deadline is met.   Righteousness exists only in the now, and living that way builds treasures that can never be taken away.

Life is a vapor, a puff of smoke that dissipates just as soon as it appears. But sometimes guys treat time like society treats oil or like the government treats money, as if it's an unlimited commodity. A wise man lives with the opposite mindset; he budgets his time wisely and always leaves a little bit aside. Then, when the inevitable unplanned event arises, he'll have time to take care of it.

Everyone knows this, so what keeps guys from using their time wisely? For some it's laziness, the sheer lack of initiative. For many, however, it takes the appearance of success.

The bottom line is that until a man defines what he truly values—and aligns his life choices to treat those things like the treasures they are—he can't live an honorable life. And without honor, lives lack meaning and fulfillment. Men get buried in minutiae. Before they know it, someone is patting them in the face with a shovel, and they realize that they have wasted the few moments God granted them on earth.

The Time-Money Equation

In the United Arab Emirates, oil money has fueled a culture where wanton displays of wealth reign as commonplace as desert dust. For the richest of the rich in this Persian Gulf country, opulence can, and often does, reach deeply into the realm of the ridiculous. With so many Ferraris and Lamborghinis on the road, the half-million-dollar cars don't do enough to identify their drivers as the privileged elite; now they've resorted to tricking out their license plates.

Single digit plates are hot sellers at auctions run by the government. At one auction, an Abu Dhabi businessman named Saeed Khouri plunked down fourteen million dollars for a piece of stamped metal embossed with the numeral one. His cousin, a stockbroker, paid nine million for the number five.[viii] Combined, their funds could have bought forty-six houses at a half million each or provided food, health care, and education for more than two thousand needy children through Operation Blessing for twenty-five years. (Don't get me started….)

Instead, these two Arab businessmen went home with a couple of rectangular pieces of metal they could bend with their bare hands. The previous record was held by Russian billionaire Roman Abramovich, who spent about a half million on the plate "VIP 1" in Great Britain in 2006. The license plates cost more than the cars they adorned, representing yet another manifestation of guys trying to prove their manhood in all the wrong ways.[ix]

It would be easy to criticize such ostentatious displays of wealth, wouldn't it? But wait, if I make fifty thousand a year and spend seventy-five dollars on a vanity plate to trick out my minivan, that's not such a big deal, right? Let's revisit Mr. Abramovich: his current fortune is estimated around $11.2 billion. Do the math: a half million bucks for a license plate is the equivalent of twenty-five dollars at my pay grade. You could say my minivan's "KWLDAD" cost me three times as much as Mr. Abramovich's plate.

But it's not about math—it's about the heart. Many believers spend a gigantic percentage of their most precious asset, their time, in activities that will do absolutely nothing for the kingdom. According to the latest stats, the average American spends more than five hours a day engaged in passive activity: television, video games, and social media on the Internet. That's about a third of your waking hours, or four months out of each year, that could be spent for the kingdom or at least doing something constructive.

Fantasy Football, Anyone?

With the rise of the Internet, the downhill trend toward passivity is getting worse. We use an hour a day surfing the Web, and — this blows my mind — more than $335 million was spent in 2009 alone, buying things that don't actually exist, so-called "virtual goods" for social media games Farmville and Mafia Wars. We're talking about purple unicorns here, people.

As for what could be done with that money, which equals out to more than a dollar per every person in America, here's some further perspective. The Southern Baptist Convention's International Mission Board had a budget of $317 million in 2009, during which its missionaries planted 24,650 churches and baptized 500,000 new believers in some of the remotest corners of the earth. In my opinion, that's a better investment than a tractor for a virtual farm.

Sometimes even the way we spend a mere buck says a whole lot about our priorities.

What Is Really Important?

If we were to administer a pop quiz to every man in your church, would they be able to name more football teams or apostles? Sports statistics or scripture? The results might be embarrassing.

It's more than embarrassing to see how many men follow their favorite passive time-waster with greater zeal than the God they claim to worship. To me that's worse than blowing fourteen million dollars on a license plate, because in the case of Sultan Saeed Khouri, the money was given to charity. The time you waste as a spectator is not.

Which is more important—my health or the time I spend watching television? Does this sound familiar? If I sit behind a desk all day, drive forty-five minutes home in rush hour traffic, then plop down in front of the flat screen with a bag of chips, what am I saying about my priorities? The funny thing is, a sedentary life is practically begging for an early grave, due to heart failure or some other stress- and obesity-related illness. Most guys know that. But why do so few choose to forgo *American Idol* to run wind sprints? We'll talk more about that in the last chapter.

Is It a Sin to be Fat?

You are not your own, for you were bought with a price. So glorify God with your body.

—1 Corinthians 6:19-20

The following fictional story is based on a compilation of several true stories and could have been mine.

Ministry was John's business. His job? To find and bring in major donors for a national Christian ministry, and he excelled at the challenge. The demanding, but extremely rewarding work gave John much satisfaction, knowing all the good being done around the world with the donations he garnered. He was often the last one in the office in the evening, due to making West Coast phone calls, and he racked up nearly 200,000 frequent flier miles each year visiting potential donors. The millions in funds he raised resulted in thousands of people coming to know Christ each year, changing their lives forever. What could be better than that?

Unfortunately, John's schedule left little time to exercise or even eat right. Over the years, his weight crept up, but he figured that was just part of getting older. As he moved into his fifties, his outlook became sort of fatalistic: God had already numbered his days, so why waste time obsessing about his cholesterol, or his waistline, or whatever? He had more important things to worry about.

One afternoon in his office John was setting up a conference call with some donors for the following week. The secretary knocked on his door to say goodbye and wish him a good weekend. When he didn't answer, she poked her head in the door and gasped. John was facedown at his desk—dead of a heart attack at age fifty-four.

His family was devastated, as was the ministry. His unexpected departure left his co-workers scrambling in the midst of a recession, the worst possible time.

But God continued to provide, and the ministry did not fail. John was sorely missed, but one might be forgiven for wondering what if. What if John had made time to take care of himself? What difference would it have made to his family? To his work? To his church? To the kingdom?

Psalm 139:16 says, "Your eyes saw my unformed substance; in your book were written, every one of them, the days that were formed for me, when as yet there was none of them."

That God knows the number of our days, however, does not absolve us of the responsibility to be good stewards of what we've been given. Just because God knows what grade you'll get on a test doesn't mean you don't need to study.

Giving everything its proper place in your life includes your health. Your body is a once-in-a-life-time gift, the only vehicle given to you in this life with which to serve and worship God. But how often do guys treat their bodies like a cheap rental car instead? Remember, the most important things are often the very things we neglect when the urgencies of life creep up on us.

Our bodies are not all of us, but they are the earth-suits God gave us to carry our souls and spirits, the tools that can turn calling and convictions into concrete actions.

More importantly, they are temples of the Holy Spirit, dwelling places that Jesus purchased with the breaking of his own body. "You were bought with a price, therefore honor God with your body." Some people contend this verse from 1 Corinthians 6 only applies to sexual purity, but a careful reading in the context of the rest of the New Testament shows this to be too narrow, I believe. (See 1 Corinthians 7:23 and 1 Corinthians 9 for more.)

If a friend loaned you his beach house for the weekend, would you trash it? God owns your body and entrusted it to you to achieve his purposes. What are you doing to maintain it?

This lesson is difficult to get through to a teenager. At that age, they usually don't have to worry about being overweight or out of shape. My sons can down pizzas and soda pop like it's an Olympic sport and never gain an ounce.

But the day will arrive when the metabolism no longer burns white-hot, and the demands of making a living might mean endless sedentary hours. When that time comes, will they have the example to look back on of their father sweating it out on a regular basis, doing the hard work of maintaining his body? Will they remember seeing Dad turn down dessert, displaying self-mastery over his appetite? They'll need to.

Look around nearly any church in the United States, and it becomes obvious that our collective discipline in this area reflects that of the society at large. In this, I believe we are missing out on one of the most powerful opportunities to demonstrate our faith to a world that desperately needs it.

Let's look at some scripture that speaks to the matter. You'll notice when the Bible speaks of discipline, it is mostly concerned with a disciplined mind. But that does *not* imply that disciplining the body isn't important. In fact, the two are irreversibly intertwined. (Italics and notations in parentheses are mine.)

Do you not know that in a race all the runners run, but only one receives the prize? So run that you may obtain it. Every athlete exercises *self-control in all things*. They do it (exercise control in all things) to receive a perishable wreath, but we (exercise control in all things to receive) an imperishable. So I do not run aimlessly; I do not box as one beating the air. But *I discipline my body and   keep it under control*, lest after preaching to others I myself should be disqualified.

— 1 Corinthians 9:24-27

We don't exercise our self-discipline for silly reasons, like to be good looking, which is a losing battle anyway. But we *do* exercise self-discipline, so that we will be models of self-control and restraint, in order to set a good example for everyone.

Many people exercise to feel better about themselves, to be more attractive, and to prolong their lives. Believers have different motivations than the world does. I want to structure my life so that I'll be equipped to do whatever God calls me to. I want to be a good steward of the health he's given me. I want to build self-discipline in small things, like staying in shape, so I'll have the fortitude to avoid the big things —like adultery. In short, I want to rip out the weeds of passivity in my life wherever they may spring up.

Coaches, how are you doing in this regard? When you look in the mirror, can you say that your body sets an example of self-discipline for your children? I'm not saying we should all look like the Greek god Adonis, but the way we take care of ourselves should demonstrate the principle set forth in the parable of the talents, namely that we should be good stewards of the resources with which God has entrusted us.

What More Valuable Resource Do You Have Than Your Health?

Ask a rich man whose health is failing if he wouldn't give up every penny to get his health back. We should never work out as if it would make God love us more. Instead, we should constantly embrace hardship in order to build a foundation of intestinal fortitude—and good health—that will enable us to serve wherever God leads.

We don't work out to prove our manhood. We work out to enable our bodies to carry out the duties of manhood. I'm not trying to be legalistic. I'm trying to be practical.

These days, it's too easy to reach a certain age and write yourself off. "Well, I'll never be the athlete I once was." For too many men, that's a cop out, an excuse to labor under out-of-whack priorities.

Maybe career pressures just don't afford time to work out. Tell that to my friend Dean Peters, whose job managing a team of computer programmers would reduce most men to blithering, sobbing wrecks within weeks. He still managed to lose over a hundred pounds by simply watching his diet and walking on his lunch break.

It can be done. And every whit of discipline a man displays is an encouragement to the people around him, especially if he is overweight. Think about it. When a fit person says, "I'm hitting the gym," nearly everyone thinks, "Show-off."

But when an "under-tall" person signs up for a 5K race, everyone gets excited and says, "You can do it!" They're secretly thinking, *Maybe I can, too!* When the Bible admonishes us to "work as unto the Lord," part of that includes working to encourage others by our example.

On the other hand, remember that, while important, your body is not *the* most important thing. A man must be ready for the moment when God calls him to lay down his life. A man will not shy away from that moment, when, as Paul writes in 2 Corinthians 5:4, "what is mortal may be swallowed up by life." There may, indeed, come defining moments when I am called to risk my life or my health for the kingdom. But John Piper puts a fine point on how we should approach those moments: we don't take risks to demonstrate our valor, but to demonstrate his value.[x]

So is being fat a sin? No, but it could be the consequence of sin. At the very least it means I should reflect on my choices, determine if they are God-honoring in this area, and ask myself if I am setting an example of mature, godly manhood.

Work With What You've Got, and Get Motivated

I'd like to make it clear after the last several paragraphs that a man should not compare himself physically to others. You were given the body you have for a purpose that fits perfectly with God's plan for your life. Everyone is given a different range of ability, and that's okay. On a business trip to Rome recently I saw a legless beggar sitting on a scrap of cardboard by the side of the road near the coliseum. If there was ever a man who could feel sorry for himself, I thought, this was the man.

Then it started to rain, and I watched as the beggar got up and hobbled away on the stumps of his missing legs. It was a sobering reminder that we should all do the best we can with what we're given, and that I, with a healthy mind and body, have no excuse not to make the most of my life.

Learning to be self-motivating is a very important part of becoming a man. Guys get motivated in different ways. For some it takes a goal—a half-marathon, for example. For others, a read-through-the-Bible plan. For many, accountability does the trick. A man must self-evaluate, figure out what motivates him, and then act to stack the deck in his favor. Writing it down helps. Maybe all it takes is to humbly ask someone close to you to be an accountability partner. Finding a buddy is very effective, but a man can't always expect someone else to take the lead. He must be willing to man up and do the right thing even if nobody else is willing to go along.

Find something that works, and *do whatever it takes*. Your life depends on it.

The Value of a Man

God created every man with a purpose, one that each can choose to fulfill or reject. When a man submits to his plan, he must set himself apart. Plan to stand out from the crowd. There should be a major difference in the lifestyle of the man who has devoted himself to God's army and the man who lives only to satisfy his own desires.

It's the difference between a cruise ship and a battleship. Both carry men across the water, but they differ greatly in form because of their intended purpose.

Paul wrote to Timothy that in every house, there are vessels designated for important tasks and those that aren't so important. In a great house there are vessels not only of gold and silver, but also of wood and clay—some for honorable use, some for dishonorable (2 Timothy 2:20).

The difference between the fine china we save for special occasions and the plasticware in which we keep the toilet brush has little to do with form but with the extrinsic value and the functionality of each vessel. The honorable man knows where his true value comes from.

Everyone wants acceptance. Guys seek it from God in lots of different ways, not realizing it has already been given. Our heavenly Father knows those desires. He created us with them, and he constantly affirms our worth as his children.

As my friend Randy Alcorn writes,

> You are a special creation of a good and all powerful God. You are the climax of his creation, the magnum opus of the greatest artist in the universe. You are created in His image, with capacities to think, feel, and worship that set you above all other life forms. You differ from the animals not simply in degree, but in kind.
>
> Not only is your kind unique, but also you are unique among your kind. God has masterminded the exact combination of DNA and chromosomes that constitute your genetic code, making you as different from all others as every snowflake differs from the rest.[xi]

When a man knows that the Creator imparts his worth and that meaning is found in the pursuit of God's purpose, there is no longer any need to look for self worth in anything else.

With God's approval, I no longer need the approval of man. This releases me to take drastic action to obey him, even in the face of ridicule. Paul wrote, "If I were still trying to please man, I would not be a servant of Christ" (Galatians 1:10).

Some guys spend their whole lives trying to impress God, as if he'd love them more if they performed like circus monkeys.

But God's love for us is unconditional. He loves you whether or not you choose to serve him. Submission self-selects a man for adventurous missions in his service, but it does not make God love him any more.

He loves you when you fail. He loves you when you succeed. God will accomplish his will with or without you. In his amazing love he wants you to join in his purpose, but God does not need a man like you. You need a God like him.

The Story of One Man

Tim Miller stood in the foyer of the White House and marveled. It was the fulfillment of a childhood dream. He was guarding the most powerful man in the world. His three years as an agent with the U.S. Secret Service had been a whirlwind of excitement, and he wondered how his career could get any better than this.

It was October 1994. He had just left the stairs leading to the President's private quarters when he heard a rapid popping sound outside and then glass shattering. Immediately, Tim's earphone crackled to life with reports from the uniformed officers outside that someone was attacking the White House. Tim sprinted to the sidewalk outside the fence. Pandemonium reigned on Pennsylvania Avenue. Secret Service officers had a man handcuffed on the ground, and thankfully, the shooting had stopped as quickly as it had begun.

It came out later that Francisco Martin Duran had remarked to friends that he was going to kill the President. No one took him seriously until he drove to Washington and, surrounded by tourists, opened fire on the President's residence with a semi-automatic assault rifle. As he stopped to change magazines, two civilians wrestled him to the ground and held him until uniformed agents arrived to arrest him. Tim took the man into custody and performed the initial interview.

Driving home that evening, Tim replayed the events in his mind. He felt good. This was right where he wanted to be—taking part in life-and-death matters of national importance, the culmination of his years as a marine and as a policeman.

Costly Success

However, he could never dispel the nagging thought that maybe the cost was just too high. Despite the incredible events of his day, his wife would be upset that he was late and had missed another family dinner. Tim loved his wife and children dearly, but all too often the family had to make do without him when duty called.

Being a Secret Service agent was all consuming— more a way of life than a job. By definition, his career took precedence when it conflicted with his personal life. Yet his family was paying a high price for his success. He worked three out of four weekends. He missed his wedding anniversary while riding camels around the Egyptian pyramids protecting a diplomat, and he missed his daughter's birthday while protecting the President in Hawaii.

But his family knew he loved them…didn't they?

Although the Secret Service chalks up the highest divorce rate of any law enforcement agency, Tim was convinced it would never happen to him and his wife LaDonna. But a knot formed in his stomach when he remembered her saying a week or two earlier, "Tim, I feel like a single parent."

Her comment confused and frustrated him. He should have been enjoying life; he was right where he had always dreamed of being. Instead, the knowledge that he was there at the expense of his wife and kids left a bitter taste in his mouth. And they weren't the ones to blame.

Time for Change

In the months following the shooting, Tim traveled more than ever. His job continued to call him to important tasks and exciting destinations. He stayed in the palace of Saudi Prince Abdullah and protected Israeli Prime Minister Rabin just three weeks before Rabin's assassination.

Then one day on his way to the White House, Tim heard Dr. James Dobson on the radio saying, "Men, if your career is causing you to miss out on your family, you need to pray and ask God to provide you a job where you can be a true husband to your wife and a good father to your children."

Those words pierced Tim's heart. In tears, he knew it was time for a drastic change. It was time for a new job. He didn't know what God had planned, but he became convinced that this was what obedience looked like for him.

Tim left the Secret Service and took another government position that allowed him to spend more time at home. His fellow agents predicted career suicide, and even Tim thought that he was making a huge sacrifice for his family. But it soon became clear that the choice to put his family ahead of his career was like trading mud for diamonds. Tim experienced greater peace and closeness to God than he had ever imagined, precisely because he stepped out on faith.

Today, Tim wouldn't trade anything for the relationships he has built with his family since he left the Secret Service. When his son Aaron got engaged, he called Tim and asked him to be his best man—an honor Tim calls, "indescribable."[xii]

Obedience Matters More Than Security

A man doesn't only sacrifice that which costs him little or nothing. A man must be willing to give up anything, even everything, to live in obedience to his calling. There is great freedom in this kind of obedience. Learning to put things in the right order isn't always comfortable or easy, but it's what a man does.

King David definitely made his share of mistakes in life, but one story near the end of his reign shows how he had matured since the days of Bathsheba. David's disobedience had brought God's judgment against Israel in the form of a plague that killed 70,000 people. Grieved at the carnage, God gives David the chance to stop the work of the death angel. He is to build an altar at a threshing floor, where the angel is stationed to carry out his mission.

When David approaches and asks to buy the plot from the threshing floor owner Araunah, he tries to honor King David by giving him the site for free—to include everything for offerings, from the oxen for the burnt offerings down to the last piece of grain—but David doesn't take the easy way out.

> But King David said to Araunah, "No, but I will buy them for the full price. I will not take for the LORD what is yours, **nor offer burnt offerings that cost me nothing.**"
>
> —2 Samuel 24:24

Being a man requires putting the most important things at the top of the list and living like the list matters. This requires making a habit of doing uncomfortable, tedious things on a regular basis. In the army we used to say, "You've got to live hard to be hard." When it comes to manhood, sometimes making life better means making it harder.

In his wild and infinite wisdom God chooses to hold men accountable in heaven, the land of unlimited time, for things done here while the clock was ticking. The honorable man knows that the time is short, that each day should be lived pursuing a profit for the kingdom. He learns to value meaning over comfort and he makes a habit of viewing everything—time, money, and work—through the lens of value.

A man of honor values things rightly.

Chapter 5

Assess and Improve

"The way to get started is to quit talking and start doing."

— Walt Disney

I had left the brokerage firm and had entered my new career as a writer, speaker, and entrepreneur, cobbling together a living from as many income sources as I could develop. As I went around the world speaking at retreats and churches on the subject of my first two books, *A More Elite Soldier* and *Bulletproof*, I started noticing a trend. At almost every event, a guy would approach me at the book table or at lunch afterward to ask for advice.

He'd start by pouring out his sad story, usually something about how his family was in shambles — his kids hated him and his wife resented him. Then he would proceed to explain how if she would just change this or that, things wouldn't be so bad.

Looking at his life as an outsider, I could easily detect some glaring point of passivity in his life that was causing the problem. I spent a lot of time wondering why these guys couldn't see that if they

took charge of something they had been neglecting in their own lives, things would improve almost overnight. More than ever, I started to understand how insidious and harmful passivity is in the lives of men.

Some of the stories I heard truly horrified me. One Christian man complained that his wife wouldn't make him supper anymore since the accident that had left her nearly paralyzed. Meanwhile, he came home from work and watched wrestling every night and expected her to keep up with the housework and shopping.

I was blown away. *How could a guy be so selfish?*

Passivity Gets Personal

Then things began to get personal. The more I saw passivity in the lives of other men, the more I started to recognize it in myself. I was reading the news on the Internet one night about nine when suddenly it felt as though my conscience whacked me with a baseball bat. I can remember the words that went through my mind as if it were yesterday.

Who is that woman?

The question tumbled around in my brain.

Who is that woman? The one upstairs right now bathing your children? Is it the same woman who has been caring for them all day long? And here you sit, leaving her to do the work, and you complain about how other men treat their wives? And you're going to complain when she has no energy left to pay attention to you tonight. Who is the selfish one?

Ouch.

The red flags began popping up almost daily--the multiple ways I was allowing passivity to creep into my life. At the same time, I was growing more and more frustrated with my writing career. I was now home all the time, but Connie pointed out that she felt more like a single parent than ever before! In reality, I wasn't "at home"; I was holed up in my home office. The problem with working for yourself, I discovered, is that the boss can be a real jerk and won't let you have any time off.

I had fallen back into the mistake of letting life's little urgencies define my mission. I had forgotten the lesson that my first job is to be obedient, not to pay the bills. The pressure to keep the lights on chained me to my desk virtually all day, every day. If the kids wanted to see me, the only view available was the back of my head as I slaved away at the computer. Not exactly what I had envisioned when I imagined the "freedom" of working for myself.

My frustration continued to grow. Business remained good, and my services, in high demand. But competing deadlines left me playing perpetual catch-up, always under the gun to finish the next big project. When I needed a little slack, I looked to my longsuffering wife and children.

Breaking the Code

It was time for drastic measures. I remembered Jesus' words in Matthew 5:29-30:

> If your right eye causes you to sin, tear it out and throw it away. For it is better that you lose one of your members than that your whole body be thrown into hell. And if your right hand causes you to sin, cut it off and throw it away. For it is better that you lose one of your members than that your whole body go into hell.

That's pretty extreme stuff. I suddenly understood the scripture to mean that big changes were sometimes required to jolt a man out of his sinful rut and get him on the right track again. That reminded me of the mindset laid out in the Ranger creed:

> Readily will I display the intestinal fortitude required to fight on to the Ranger objective and complete the mission though I be the lone survivor. [xiii]

A man must do whatever it takes to be obedient, no matter what. But what did that look like in my life today? I came to understand that the source of my frustration lay in points of passivity that had a foothold in my life. Breaking the code would come down to my ability to root them out and eliminate them.

Assess and Improve

Everyone has an Uncle Keith, I think.

You know, the guy who knows how to do just about everything? The one who has been gainfully employed since he was about four years old? He's the guy whose picture you see when you look up the term *jack-of-all-trades* in the dictionary.

My uncle Keith is just like that. I love it when he comes to visit, because he always fixes things. It doesn't matter if it's his only week of vacation for the year; he'd rather be replacing the leaky plumbing in our master bathroom than sitting on the couch watching football. Or hanging sheetrock in the addition we've been working on for a year. The last time he came to visit, he tightened all the hinges on the cabinets in my kitchen.

Watching Uncle Keith, I learned an important lesson about manhood. A man continually looks at his environment and thinks of ways to make it better. Men view situations with an eye to fix what is broken and create value. And once they've assessed, men take action—whether as insignificant as picking up a burger wrapper off the ground or as daring as rescuing someone from an oncoming bus—to make things better for everybody.

A man who makes a habit of constantly acting on the impulse to make things better will never lack for profitable work. He'll never have to worry about not being able to find something to do or how to provide for his family, because a man who consistently improves himself and the lives of others is reflecting God's glory, which is his highest purpose.

Those men have discovered that happiness is found by leading others to it.

It Starts With Me

This assess-improve process starts with the guy in the mirror. If I don't measure the way I spend my days, I can't change anything. It's often easier to see where others need to improve than to see where I fall short, but it has to start with me. I can't control what others choose to do (and, indeed, I shouldn't try), but I can change myself.

Most people find self-evaluation difficult. It's like trying to watch yourself blink in a mirror. I've found one simple, if sometimes painful method: ask a spouse, sibling, parent, or best friend where I need to improve. Those who love me the most have the most personal interest in helping me become better. Setting my ego aside is usually the most difficult part. After that, improvement comes fairly easily.

Other methods not as embarrassing might yield useful information. Rescuetime.com is a free software program that sends out a weekly summary of my online habits. I am sometimes shocked to find how much time I waste there on things that aren't especially profitable. A few days of keeping record of how my time is spent pay big dividends. How much time do I spend driving, sleeping, watching television, checking email? Extrapolating those numbers into a yearly figure helped me realize that I wasn't wasting minutes...it was more like months. That kind of eye-opening exercise, for me, is often just the kind of motivation I need to make a change.

How about a one-month experiment? I like the concept of "fasting" from the biggest time-wasters I can identify in my life. Almost always, my stress level drops and relationships improve.

If anything is true about the human male, it's that we don't like to admit our weaknesses. A man must become an expert at doing just that. A man knows that there is no profit in deceiving himself. My heart often tries to deceive me — to tell me it would be impossible or too expensive to make the changes that need to be made. But if I'm going to call myself a man, I must be willing to admit to my weaknesses and failures. When I do, their power over me is broken.

When I sat down and took a long, honest look at how I spent my time, the result was…liberation. Well, shock, dismay, and embarrassment came along for the ride, but I found that laying out all my habits and proclivities in the light made it easier to sort through them and decide what needed to go.

In the last chapter we learned how to distinguish honorable things from dishonorable. If a better understanding of value helps illuminate the difference between a flower and a weed, assessment is actually walking between the furrows of the garden to determine which plants must be removed, which must be pruned, and which must be fed and cultivated. Then it's time to get out the hoe—or chainsaw, as the case may be.

If there are clanking and grinding sounds coming from the car's engine, just turning up the stereo will never fix the problem. Having problems in your life is not a sign of weakness. Refusing to act to make things better is.

The Definition of Passivity

If you're going to hunt deer, it's a good idea to learn to distinguish the difference between a ten-point buck and, say, your neighbor's Great Dane. In the same way, a solid definition of *passivity* is crucial to the man who is resolved to hunt it down and eliminate it from his life.

Passivity is more than laziness. It's more than inactivity. Believe it or not, passivity can look like strutting tough guy bravado as easily as it can resemble a TV-watching lump on the couch.

The root of passivity goes back to the gateway to manhood: submission. When a guy fails to submit any part of his life to the purpose for which he was created, he is being passive. He's failing to live up to his calling as a man. That is passivity.

You can learn a lot about a word by studying its antonym, the opposite meaning. So what is the opposite of passivity? Activity? Not necessarily. Moral courage? That's getting closer.

A man will be passionate about fulfilling his role in life. That passion engenders the power to do so. And a powerful man differs from the passive guy in this way—his submission to God's purpose gives him the ability to fulfill his calling in life. Therefore, the opposite of passivity is passion and power.

You Are Your Own Worst Enemy

Passivity exists any time a guy fails to live up to his calling. Whether he's failing to be the spiritual leader for his family or failing to submit to the authority placed over him, passivity reveals a failure to do one's duty, whatever that might be. Every man struggles with it—our culture makes sure of that. Today's world works to encourage passivity in men at every turn. The messages are continual: enjoy yourself, take it easy, relax, avoid risky behavior.

We are bombarded with all sorts of activity designed to keep us from actually doing anything meaningful. We are constantly encouraged to gratify ourselves, to watch others' make-believe lives on TV, while we sit on our couches and let ours slip away. The sad thing? This life-sucking waste of time has become so commonplace that not engaging in those passive pastimes makes others see you as a freak or at least an uncultured boob. The whole system is set up to suck the life out of you before you do something drastic or even meaningful.

For the short time I'm given on earth, I don't ever want to simply pass time. I want to invest it.

As if our cowardly culture didn't make being a man difficult enough, passivity also wells up from within, a gift from our forefather Adam. Resisting passive activity is only a start. I must always be on the lookout for traitors within my own camp.

In the army I learned how easy it was to get off course when walking across the slope of a hill. The downward pull of gravity would throw a guy off his azimuth, so we were taught to intentionally maintain an upward bias in situations like that in order to maintain a straight line. Upward to go straight? You got it.

Minds work that way, too. They obey the law of entropy, which says that the universe tends toward disorder. Keeping the status quo is not keeping a straight line. There is a steady tide that pulls a man toward uselessness that must be resisted. This goes back to the concept of intentionally making your life harder for the purpose of making yourself better.

When mechanics inspect cars, they look for points of friction that keep the engine from running smoothly. Passivity is like that—sand in the gears of a healthy life. A man needs to regularly sit down with paper and pen and list all the places—relationally, spiritually, emotionally, financially, and physically—that could use a little oil.

Where am I engaging in passive activity?
Where am I failing to protect my family?
Where am I valuing things more than people?
Where do I have ruts in my life?
What weeds need to be rooted out and thrown away?
When was the last time I took a risk and trusted God with the outcome?

In May of 2003, the news told the amazing story of a lone climber named Aron Ralston, whose arm was crushed by a falling boulder. He was trapped for several days. Dehydrated, hungry, and hurting with the wound growing infected, he decided his only chance for survival was to break his upper arm bone and use a three-inch pocket knife to saw through the decaying flesh in order to wriggle free.

I shudder even to think what that must have been like. The excruciating physical pain and the mental anguish of separating a limb from one's own body are tough to think about. But for Aron the choice was clear: live without an arm or don't live at all.

Maybe the issues most men struggle with aren't so cut and dried—pardon the pun. Maybe there is trouble with a relationship or with the boss at work, or maybe the problem is one that nobody else sees. Whatever it is, a man has to be ferociously honest, at least with himself, and figure out what's holding him back that needs to get cut off—no matter how painful.

If You Own the Blame, You Can Change the Game

Jared's marital problems centered on one issue: his wife was spending them into bankruptcy. He worked hard to provide for her, but no matter how much he made, she managed to find a way to spend a little more. What could he do? They often fought over money. When he confronted her, the conversation quickly turned nuclear. To call her a "shopping addict in full-blown denial" would have been an understatement. Jared loved his wife, but after seven years the marriage had unraveled to the point he started giving serious consideration to leaving. Even the thought of divorce hurt, especially since they now had a ten-month-old baby. But he had tried everything he knew to make her happy, or so he believed. Divorce loomed as the only remaining option.

Jared and I had been friends for a long time. I'm no marriage counselor, but he came to me for advice. After listening to his side of the story, I saw the obvious answer.

I looked him in the eye and said, "I hate to tell you this, Buddy, but this is all your fault."

Jared's shocked expression let me know that wasn't the help he was expecting. I asked him not to punch me until I had a chance to explain, and he agreed, albeit, with difficulty.

The problem, as I saw it, was that Jared did not love his wife the right way. Any married man wants to make his wife happy, but the more loving thing to do is to help her be *good*, not *feel* good. A man is called to *lead* his family. A leader says, "This is the way we're going to go … follow me." Leadership often requires making tough decisions that, in the heat of the moment, might get you called things like "unreasonable"…or worse.

Jared had been indulging, even enabling, his wife's addiction for years in a losing bid to appease her. By not stepping up to say "enough," Jared was actually neglecting his wife, resulting in her feeling resentful and dissatisfied. Shopping served as an outlet for her frustration.

My advice? Jared should decide on an amount he could afford to let his wife spend and then tell her the following:

"Honey, I need to apologize for what has happened lately in our marriage. I have been giving you everything except what you really need, which is help in controlling your spending. As the man of this house, I have a responsibility to you and to our baby. It is part of my job to provide for us and lead our home spiritually, and at that I have failed. I want to ask for your forgiveness. I was wrong, but I'm going to make it right, and I hope you can find it in your heart to trust me.

"For the time being, because of our financial situation, things are going to be tight around here. I am not going to hide money from you or keep you out of the loop in any way regarding our finances.

In order to make it easier to get this accomplished, I'm going to give you two hundred dollars per month to spend any way you like. Buy purses, get your nails done, whatever. I will take care of everything else— even the grocery shopping, if necessary. The money I give you is yours to spend, but that is all we can spare for you until the first of next month."

Jared laughed in my face. "Are you kidding? She'll go ballistic! She'll probably even leave."

"The truth is," I answered, "you can't *make* her stay no matter what you do. You can only control *you*. If she chooses to leave, tell her you wish she would stay, but stick to your guns about the finances. See what happens."

He called me a week later, incredulity ringing in his voice. "I had the talk with my wife," he said. "It was ugly at first, just like I thought it would be. But after the dust settled a few days later, I noticed something amazing. She actually seems relieved!"

I might have been exaggerating when I told Jared it was entirely his fault. But not by much. The truth is, the only thing a man can change about a problem is the part that he controls. So he learns to look for points of passivity in his own life when confronting a problem and then takes drastic action to get rid of them.

Often, that's all that is necessary to bring change in those around him.

Just Do It

"So whoever knows the right thing to do and fails to do it, for him it is sin" (James 4:17).

A compass does not work in your pocket. You'll never bag that trophy buck that wanders into your sights if you only aim at it. At some point, you have to pull the trigger.

Assessment is the easiest part of the process, but if a guy doesn't follow through and improve the situation, nothing changes.

A man must be willing to take drastic action to change his life if he perceives he is falling into an unhealthy rut. A man does whatever it takes to do what is right. Anyone can do the right thing when it's easy and safe. A man does what's right when it's difficult, costly, and dangerous. That's what sets him apart.

You're the Man. Now Act Like It.

They are sorry excuses, but guys use them all the time: "It's not my fault" or "It's none of my business."

How many times have you heard someone say, "It's not my job to...pick up that trash, mow that lawn, discipline that child..." or any of a thousand other copouts. It's sad, but I guess we shouldn't expect much more from a species that's been passing the buck since the beginning. Adam committed the first act of passivity by giving up his role as head of the family and "hearkening to his wife." He went on to rationalize his subsequent sin by placing the blame squarely on Eve and indirectly on God. "The man said, 'The woman *you* put here with me...she gave me some fruit from the tree, and I ate it'" (Genesis 3:12).

Men don't play such games. They take responsibility for where things stand in each area of their lives, no matter how it happened. Even if it isn't their fault.

But how can I take ownership over a wrong that I didn't commit or a dilemma I didn't cause?

Change the things you can control, and leave the rest up to God. The blame game never has a winner. Whether you dug the ditch or simply fell into it, the next step is the same: climb out of the hole. Get busy and leave the finger pointing to someone else.

Does this mean a man puts on false humility and grovels about wrongs that he didn't commit? Not at all. A man simply stays focused on the objective and allows God to mold him into the man he needs to be.

He leaves the worry about whose fault it is to someone else. Very often that process will change more than the man—it will also change the world around him.

Excuses, Excuses

In the book of Genesis, the boy named Joseph had to learn to assess and improve even though initially things didn't go his way. Once the favorite child of his father Jacob, Joseph demonstrated immaturity combined with a sense of destiny to stir up jealousy among his brothers. One day they'd finally had enough. They threw him into a hole and then sold him into slavery in Egypt. He lost everything—possessions, relationships, even his identity.

But God had a plan for Joseph.

Once in a new land, Joseph found his life didn't exactly get better right away. Wrongly accused of attempted rape, he was thrown into jail, where he languished for more than two years before getting a chance to win back his freedom. Through his God-given ability to interpret dreams, he eventually ascended to Pharaoh's court and became Egypt's second in command.

Joseph didn't achieve this high position by lamenting about the unfairness he faced in the world. He was always looking for ways to make things better. In his first post, he managed the household so well that his master entrusted him with everything. Once in jail, the overseer put him in charge of the rest of the inmates. When he made it to Pharaoh's house, his leadership earned him a position of control over the whole country. Joseph didn't whine when things went south, which showed he was learning the way of manhood. He didn't make excuses.

God's favor had everything to do with Joseph's ascent, but that worked in tandem with Joseph's submission to God's plan and his mature response to hardship. Rather than whine about everything wrong, he worked to make everything better. He knew he was called to be an instrument of God's redemptive power in the world. He viewed difficulty not as a sign that God didn't love him, but as an indicator that God wanted to use him. Joseph learned that God puts men in
dark situations, so that they can shine and reflect the grace and glory of their Creator.

Matthew 5:16 puts it this way:

> In the same way, let your light shine before others, so that they may see your good works and give glory to your Father who is in heaven.

Created to Rule

Unlike Joseph, many men fail to make the most of their lives, because they allow passivity and negativity to cloud their purpose. But here's truth: no matter what your situation, if you woke up this morning, God has a plan for you. The world you live in isn't heaven…that comes later. For the time being, let's get busy. There's a lot of work to be done.

The truth about God's plan for men is revealed in the opening pages of scripture. When God created and placed him in the garden, he said, "Let us make man in our image, after our likeness. And let them have dominion…" (Genesis 1:26).

Man's main purpose is to be the glory bearer, the reflection of God's image on earth. The Bible goes on to say in Genesis 1:28, "And God blessed them." In this context the word *blessed* indicates that he set mankind apart for a special purpose, the vehicle through which God would complete his plan for the world.

God is always creating, shepherding, blessing, redeeming, and protecting his family. Jesus modeled what that looks like on earth. He used his God-power to heal the sick and raise the dead—big things. And he used his carpenter's hands to make furniture and cuddle a child—little things.

Men are called to reflect his glory, and that is accomplished by modeling his character. They follow Jesus by improving the world in big and small ways: saving lives, standing up for the defenseless, and being the best accountant, plumber, soldier, student, father, or son they can be. Men are most like Christ when they are loving, leading, blessing, and protecting the people around them.

A boy picks up the mantle of manhood whenever he decides to do those things. That's what a man was made to do. Age is irrelevant. Unfortunately, there are so few who do it.

Passivity Hunting

As I mentioned in Chapter 1, I started reading through the Bible with an eye specifically toward male passivity. The stories jumped out at me right away. Adam remained passive in the garden when he allowed Eve to take and eat the fruit. I previously never realized he was actually there with her when the serpent tempted her. I'd always assumed the first sin was Eve's, but perhaps this is why Adam is credited with bringing sin into the world in Romans 5:12. It says:

Therefore, just as sin came into the world through one man, and death through sin, and so death spread to all men because all sinned.

One wonders what would have been different if Adam had stepped up and fulfilled his duty to protect Eve.

Eli was passive with his sons and failed to do his duty in raising them right. As a consequence, his sons suffered and died by the hand of a holy God. With three boys of my own, that one hits close to home.

Even King David, my Bible hero since I was a child, allowed passivity to wreak havoc in his family. His sin didn't begin with Bathsheba, but earlier, before he saw the beautiful woman bathing on her rooftop. The story recounts that it was the spring of the year, "when kings go off to war." Time to shore up the border fences, so to speak. But then it goes on to say that while David's troops were serving in the field, their commander-in-chief was sitting on his couch back at the castle. There, in that failure to lead his men from the front, we see the sin that led to David's failure with Bathsheba.

Contrast that with her husband Uriah, the Hittite. A man with a high sense of honor, he knew a leader should never seek comfort while his men were miserable, and he refused to sleep in his own bed when summoned back to Jerusalem by King David. Imagine how the sight of Uriah sleeping on his porch must have convicted King David.

Passivity, the failure to do one's duty as a man in any area, is like toxic waste; it poisons a man's relationships and harms everything in his path. I made a decision to hunt down and eliminate every shred of passivity from my life. But I had no idea how much that resolution would change everything.

Step one to killing off the passivity in my life was a brutal self-assessment. I sat down with a pencil and broke my life down into six primary areas:

- Spiritual
- Family
- Physical
- Mental/Academic
- Financial
- Career

At first glance, I concluded I wasn't an outright failure in any of these areas, so that was a start...and a relief...

- I read my Bible almost every day.
- Because I worked from home, my wife and kids saw more of me than most families.
- I wasn't grossly overweight or out of shape.
- I read more than most men.
- We weren't starving or behind on our bills.
- My career as a writer was progressing and had branched out into television and public speaking.

I was feeling pretty good about myself when it hit me: I was feeling good, because I was comparing myself to most guys instead of the true standard. The standard of "most guys" wasn't my target. My goal was zero passivity, and as I took a second glance at my life, I was horrified to find areas of passivity almost everywhere.

Point of Passivity #1: Spiritual

I was failing at my responsibility to be the pastor to my family. Sure, I kept a quiet time, but my responsibility as a man went much further. Deuteronomy 6 tells me that my job includes teaching God's commands to my children and leading my family spiritually to reflect God's love to the world. I had some work to do in that department.

Point of Passivity #2: Family

I might have been present in the house more than most men, but, as I mentioned earlier, I was confusing quantity with quality. I had a problem with shutting off my work brain and really *being there* for my kids. I needed to make changes to show them how very precious they were to me.

Point of Passivity #3: Physical

I might not have been a big slob, but sitting at a desk for more than ten years had begun to send me in that direction. I was not taking care of my body as I should and then justifying it almost as a point of pride. I used my expanding gut as proof of how hard I worked. Truth indicated otherwise; I was just lazy. Maybe I didn't have to look like Adonis, but I should at least look like I give a rip about the vehicle on loan to me by my Creator—the only one given me to glorify Him here on earth.

Point of Passivity #4: Mental/Academic

Most men read an average of one book per year once they leave college. I knew that if I was serious about "working as unto the Lord" at my career, I needed to read a lot more than that. Comparing myself to everyone else was just a copout.

Point of Passivity #5: Financial

Finding the passivity in my finances was more challenging than the other areas of my life. Our bills were getting paid. Good enough, right? Then I realized I was concentrating on how much I was making, but there's a whole lot more to finances than that. How much were we giving? Wouldn't our generosity be a better indicator of financial health? Also, Connie was the one who did the bills, so I assumed we were at least tithing. But then it hit me: I didn't know how much we were giving. Heck, I didn't know how much we spent on electricity or groceries every month. Since Connie was the detail person, I'd always left the checkbook to her.

However, one of the responsibilities of manhood is being the liaison between one's family and the world. To be honest, I was leaving Connie to face the bill collectors, while I was hiding behind the fact that she was the detail person. The turning point came when I noticed a situation   close to home. Whenever we received a call from the tenants in our rental to let us know the rent would be late, it was always the wife who called. Often, I'd hear the husband in the background saying, "Tell him I get paid next Friday!" Which made me sorely tempted to tell the woman, "Why don't you put that coward of a husband on the phone, so he can tell me himself?"

But in a sense, I was doing the same thing.

As I delved into our finances, I saw how stressful it must have been for my wife to keep track of everything. When I needed something and there was money in the account, I bought it. I rarely thought about the tough position that might put Connie in when she went to pay the bills. But come to think of it, our disagreements often revolved around money. It quickly became clear I needed to take over the finances. At first Connie was angry; she felt   as though I were firing her. I tried to explain my thought processes, but she still felt slighted. I stuck to my guns, though, and a few months later she came to me and thanked me for releasing her from that burden.

She hadn't fully realized the stress that situation had caused in our marriage, and indeed, we rarely fought about money anymore. I'm sure I'm less efficient in getting everything paid on time, but I have certainly gained a new respect and appreciation for what my wife endured.

Point of Passivity #6: Career

At that time the biggest frustration in my life came from the peak I was pointing to as the symbol of my success—my career. My dissatisfaction stemmed from the constant challenge of competing elements—from book deadlines to speaking opportunities. Churches around the country invited me to speak to their men's groups. How could I pass up a chance to minister to others? Though crushed by looming book deadlines, I knew my books were touching lives, so it had to be God's will, right? The television reports I made were also impacting lives. But the more that opportunities came my way, the more I began to resent them. It felt as though everyone wanted a piece of me, leaving only crumbs of time and attention for the things that mattered most—my family, my church, and my health. So many little urgencies popped up every day that I started to believe it wasn't possible to live my priorities. That depressing thought only increased my disgruntlement.

Eventually the frustration grew so acute I couldn't take it anymore. Looking back, I think I actually resented God and even blamed him for telling me to live priorities that looked impossible.

I knew that if I was going to shed the insidious passivity creeping into every corner of my life, I needed to take drastic measures. And I needed to do it soon.

Chapter 6
Perish and Provide

The ultimate measure of a man is not where he stands in moments of comfort and convenience. But where he stands at times of challenge and controversy.

—Martin Luther King, Jr.

Army Ranger Benjamin Kopp was younger than most college seniors when he faced his third tour of duty in Afghanistan. After passing the grueling physical and mental tests required for becoming a Ranger, the handsome twenty-one-year-old left family, friends, and comfort to protect his country and bring freedom to an unfamiliar people in a dusty foreign land. While many of his peers back home hung out in dorm rooms playing the *Call of Duty* video game, Kopp was answering that call in the real world, beating back resilient Taliban fighters on hostile ground. He served in the 3rd battalion of the 75th Ranger regiment, which was my unit in the early 1990s.

One summer day a sizable enemy force attacked another Special Operations team in that area, and the team called for backup. Kopp and his team responded to get them out. Attacking across a wide, open area under intense enemy fire, Kopp and his squad kept the Taliban fighters' heads down long enough for the Special Ops team to withdraw.

Kopp and his men then began to pull back themselves; Ben insisted on staving off the enemy with his squad automatic weapon until the rest of his men made it to safety. In the midst of the gunfire, Corporal Kopp took a bullet in the leg, puncturing his femoral artery. Although he was rushed from the battlefield into surgery, loss of blood caused him to go into cardiac arrest on the operating table. He was transported to Walter Reed Army Medical Center in Washington, D.C., where he lingered for several days, before dying July 18, 2010.

Men Perish to Their Own Desires to Provide for the Needs of Others

Kopp's sacrifice galvanized his brothers in arms and provided a poignant reminder of the heroism of our brave soldiers. But for a fifty-seven-year-old woman in Chicago, his death achieved something even more valuable: a chance at a new life.

Earlier Benjamin Kopp had indicated his desire to be an organ donor, so his heart, liver, kidneys, and pancreas were all removed and donated, along with skin tissue. Judy Meikle, a friend of Kopp's cousin, had been on the transplant list for seventy-seven days. Benjamin's mother, Jill Stephenson, designated Meikle as the recipient of her son's heart, but nothing guaranteed that the young Ranger's heart would match hers.

Miraculously, the heart of the Minnesota-born soldier proved to be a match for Meikle, who had a rare form of congenital heart failure. She recovered quickly after the successful operation and was soon able to resume her life.

Judy Meikle remains grateful over the amazing trade of her weary ticker for one less than half its age, but not only for the vibrant new muscle tissue. She also treasures the fact that every beat of her heart brings a thumping reminder of the power of sacrifice. Kopp's courage and selfless service on the battlefield proved his heroism, and with one final act of caring, he saved yet another life.

In death, the corporal exemplified another essential characteristic of manhood: in a world that rewards those who put self first, men act differently.[xiv]

Boys Take, Men Give

On the outside, it's easy to tell when a male child begins turning into an adult. When puberty hits, the voice drops in pitch, muscles fill out, hair grows in unfamiliar places—you know the drill.

Unfortunately, for many guys, a fuzzy armpit is about all that separates them from the chubby-cheeked pipsqueaks they were before puberty. Pastor Mark Driscoll calls them "boys who can shave." They look like men, but their behavior changes little. They remain passive, irresponsible, and self-indulgent. They spend inordinate amounts of time playing games and approach every situation with one question: "Where's the fun?"

A boy takes. A man gives. Those telling statements easily determine when a boy has taken up the mantle of manhood. When you become a man, it's no longer about you. It's about providing for the needs of others. A man doesn't act like he deserves to be catered to or needs to be happy, comfortable, or rich.

Look at how a guy spends his time, energy, and resources. How much of his attention is drawn to things centered on entertainment? How often does he forgo personal pleasure for the subtler delight of doing his duty before God?

It isn't chin stubble, a voting card, or a tattoo that distinguishes a boy from a man. It's his attitude. A boy says, "Somebody ought to do something."
A man says, "I can do it." A boy says, "What's in it for me?" A man says, "How can I help?"

Whether it's picking up the dirty laundry or breaking up a fistfight in the street, a boy becomes a man when he stops focusing on his own wants and starts focusing on what others need. It's how he treats family, friends, and even the stranger on the street. He displays a willingness to sacrifice fleeting joys to ensure that good comes to those he loves—and even to his enemies.

We begin our lives clothed in self-indulgence. From birth, children are preoccupied with themselves. Totally dependent upon their parents, they care about nothing but their own desires.

Growing up requires that we reverse this pattern. Being a man compels boys to become producers, not just consumers; contributors, not just spectators.

On my latest trip to Kenya, I stayed with a missionary family that employs a teenager to work on the family's home. Narasha proved to be a good worker, and the missionaries pay him an above-average wage in a country with widespread poverty and unemployment. Still, he never buys anything for himself. Every cent he makes goes toward one goal: putting a thatched roof on his mother's house to help shelter her and the other five children she's raising without the help of a husband.

Although only fourteen, Narasha is a man. Nobody told him to think of his mother and to forfeit the joys of a carefree adolescence in order to meet his family's basic needs.

He exemplifies a life of sacrifice, simply because it needs to happen.

Like Narasha and Corporal Kopp, men don't wait to fulfill their duties until they bring personal benefit. Where there is lack, they provide. No questions asked.

What Men Do

Then He said to them all, "If anyone would come after me, let him deny himself and take up his cross daily and follow me" (Luke 9:23).

In putting away every cent to provide for his mother's roof, Narasha emulates Christ. The Bible says that Jesus was fully God but made himself a man for our sakes. Then he gave everything he had to take away our guilt before the Father. When a man puts the needs of others before his own, he reflects God's goodness to the world. But wasn't it easy for Jesus? After all, he was God! True, but he was also man. Gethsemane shows us the profound burden that he faced in submission.

This story comes from a message board posting on a Web site I maintain for small farmers. It was written by the wife of a man who demonstrated manhood by providing for the needs of others:

My husband often gave the response, "That's what a man does." That was always his reply when I'd talk to him about going to work when he didn't feel well, or when he worked a simply rotten job because we needed the money for bills, or when he was the calm in the eye of the storm, "That's what a man does."

The 19th of this month we buried my husband. At the funeral home, I saw one fellow standing beside the casket, holding on to it...looking like he was going to faint. My daughter went over to him and started talking, so I continued talking to one of my husband's friends.

A few minutes later my daughter brought the man over to me and said, "Mom, this man has a story you need to hear."

Part of the story I knew. More than a decade before, my husband had worked with this man, when the man's wife had just given birth to twins. The premature boys had many medical issues and were just barely holding on.

The boys needed individual alarm systems that would alert the parents when their breathing or hearts stopped. Insurance would pay for only one alarm, and the young family needed money to get an alarm for the
second twin. The parents were staying up night and day, trying to keep both boys alive. My husband told me he was able to help them some; that's all I ever knew.

The rest of the story...somehow, my husband was able to convince enough people so that he was able to walk up to the father of the twins one day not long after learning of the parents' need, lay down a check for $32,000 and say, "I hope this helps." The check managed to pay not only for the needed machine, but also for nursing help in the parents' home.

The man told me his twin sons are eleven years old, now—intelligent, healthy, active, growing like weeds, and sure to be a good six-foot tall.

I never did know the extent my husband had helped the family. Dave wasn't one to brag about the good things he did, and I doubt he ever mentioned it to anyone else either.

He just did what a man does and moved on.[xv]

What Men Don't Do

Sadly, for every man who gets this concept, there will be a hundred guys who don't have a clue. They've bought into the lie that becoming a man means everyone else is supposed to serve you, that "rank has its privileges."

I knew Louis for a long time. We attended the same men's Bible study group, which we cultivated as a place of openness and accountability. But Louis was hiding a skeleton he believed was too ghastly to reveal even in the presence of his closest Christian brothers.

We never suspected anything. Lou was an upstanding member of the community who seemed to have a normal family life. His two teenagers and wife of eighteen years seemed happy in the home that Lou's labor had provided. That is, until the bomb dropped.

One day Lou's wife, with one of their children, returned home unexpectedly and found him in bed with another man. From all accounts, it was like a scene from a bad TV drama, with shouting, weeping, and gnashing of teeth. He was caught. His family was devastated. And life as they knew it would never again be the same.

What happened next only made things worse. For a guy who had spent years taking his family to church, Lou did not show the slightest contrition.

Instead he appeared to be relieved that he no longer needed to hide his perversion. "I've been providing for this family for nearly twenty years," he said. "Now it's my turn to be happy."

Your turn? Really? Does a man put his own happiness before that of his family? Lou's hardheartedness revealed just how much of a detour his heart had taken. Happiness had become his god, at the expense of his duty before the Creator of the universe. As his home fell apart, Lou moved in with his new lover, renounced his faith, and tried to convince himself and his shattered family that this was all normal.

Lou was trying to get his needs met for affirmation and affection, but he wanted to do it his way. His sin was an escape, a rebellion against the duties of family life. And even if moving in with another man is the one thing that would never happen to you, every guy is vulnerable to the same sense of self-entitlement that led to the destruction of Lou's family. Lou gave in to the lie that he deserved to indulge himself rather than to live up to his calling as a man.

He also gave in to a more subtle deception: that provision is simply putting food on the table, buying school supplies, or showing up for baseball games and ballet recitals. These are the basics, but it takes a lot more to cultivate a marriage or raise a child. Imagine the ire of a wife whose patronizing husband believes he has fulfilled his duty by simply paying the bills.

Provision is financial, yes, but it's also emotional and spiritual. It means providing for all needs, material and immaterial.

When a man is called to marry, the commitment he makes to that one special daughter of God is more than, "I will love you until I change my mind" or "I will love you as long as you make me feel good" or "I will love you until you stop being attractive." This isn't a dog we're talking about. His commitment must be, "I will love you and give my life to you, and if necessary, give up my life for you." This doesn't just mean he'll dive in front of a bus to save her. It means he'll stay with her and give her his undivided devotion *even if* she no longer makes him feel good. *Even if* she stops being attractive. *Even if* she stops loving him back.

The magic of a commitment like that is that once it's made, it frees that woman to return his love in ways he never thought possible. The shared joys and heartaches experienced together make her seem sweeter and more beautiful with each passing year. I know. I've been married to Connie almost two decades, and my biggest regret today is that I didn't marry her sooner.

Why? I've come to the conclusion that if I get eighty years with this woman, it won't be near enough.

You can have a marriage like that. But you have to die to get it—die to your selfish desires and live up to your calling as a man.

Let me make this perfectly clear: *you don't deserve to be happy.* Let me say it again. Despite what the world around you may say, *you do not have a right to happiness.*

The Paradox of Manhood

The world inundates us with advertisements that promise the kind of luxurious experiences we "deserve." It's bent on persuading us that there is some cosmic benevolence to be tapped simply through positive thinking--that everyone is naturally good and should expect good things. The media simultaneously portrays manhood as a melancholy group of metrosexuals or a bunch of Cro-Magnons burping and scratching at the football game without a care in the world. Let the women worry about being responsible. You're a man!

I don't know what planet those ideas came from, but on planet earth it doesn't work that way. If you're a Christian, Jesus calls you to a life of constant sacrifice to help fix the broken pieces of a once perfect world that was shattered by sin.

He calls you to shine his light into dark places and to live in such a dangerous way that people will be amazed at the way he cares for his own.

To take part in God's drama, a man learns the joy of suffering for a purpose bigger than himself. He puts to death the selfish little boy who thinks life is all about fun and about being entertained—whose personal security is the end-all and be-all of his existence. To become a man, he can no longer drive to work and back home in a stupor, unaware of the brokenness around him on every side. He no longer retains the luxury of ignoring the world's cries for help.

A man enlists in God's army. And every soldier must learn that comfort will get you killed.

Jake once played a role in the battle. A seminary-trained pastor, he led a church of about 80 people in a rural community. In addition to his duties as a clergyman, he worked full-time at a correctional institution to provide for his family. Eventually, the stress of two jobs and a rebellious son eroded his resolve and self-confidence, leaving him exposed to the snipers of the enemy. He was caught with a woman who was not his wife, a woman in the church whose marriage ceremony he had performed a few years earlier. Jake was forced to resign in disgrace. He too had fallen for the lie that he deserved to be happy. In believing that lie, he made himself, his family, and the whole community very *unhappy*.

The battlefield is littered with men like Lou and Jake, who gave up their role in the kingdom and their responsibility to provide because they were not willing to perish to their own desires. To put self first persists as a common temptation that every guy has to battle. No one likes to put off pleasure. Putting ourselves last goes against everything that our bodies and minds are programmed to do.

Yet living for myself leaves me empty. When I bring safety, happiness, and comfort to others, even at the expense of short-term gain, the sacrifice doesn't sting for long. Any sacrifices come back to me in greater measure. This is not karma. This is the way God structured our hearts. We are fulfilled when we fill others. A man must learn that happiness can't be hunted down like a trophy buck. It's one of those things that will come to you—as soon as you quit chasing it.

Paradoxically, self-denial brings more joy in the long run. Maximized joy. God designed us in such a way that we must look outward—and ultimately heavenward—to be fulfilled.

Happiness is obtained by giving it away. To die is to live. That's the paradox of manhood.

Your Life Is Over

The ritual of the bachelor party marks the passage of a man into that fraternity of married men whose lives, as they once knew them, are over. Groomsmen, often unfettered themselves, plan a wild night of partying, casting it as the groom's last chance to live freely before being shackled to a wife's ball and chain.

In a sense, they're right. When a man marries, his freedom, if defined as living without obligation to another, is over. You are no longer your own man. You now hold a lifelong responsibility to take care of the daughter of God whom you have chosen. No other woman can enter your mind or arms. You are charged with leading your wife into a deeper fellowship with God. You will no longer reign as supreme. You have to share your home and give up all your secrets. When a dirty or dangerous situation comes along, you are the one charged to take care of it. That's what a man does.

Many guys see this transition as the end of an era, a funeral for their singleness. Our society portrays losing one's "independence" as emasculating. But those on the path to manhood view marriage as a gate, not a cliff. Voluntarily giving your life to your wife is designed to be the ultimate emulation of Christ's love for the church. This means "fun" drops to the bottom of the list.

Fun, after all, is a poor facsimile of fulfillment. If men are to be caretakers, leaders, and providers, we must shoulder the mantle of responsibility. A man embraces the challenge and steps into this role with boldness.

Of course, family life offers the easiest example of a man's decision to provide, but it's not the only one. Men make a habit of providing for the needy around them. My friend Mike has never been called to marry, but he has fulfilled the role of provider where God has placed him, in a community with a military base near his home. He started a citywide singles Bible study and has mentored dozens of young soldiers. With several advanced degrees, Mike could surely be making more money at a prestigious college in a big city, but he has instead answered the call to be there for our military personnel. In so doing, Mike has become a hero to heroes.

Become a mentor. Provide for a widow or orphan. Help a homeless person. Let someone stay in your home temporarily. Do some yard work for a sick or elderly neighbor. Pray about the many ways you can take hold of God's call to perish and provide. In fact, putting off this facet of manhood until you take a wife only shows you aren't ready to be married. Take on someone else's burden, and you'll show you are the kind of man worth marrying. In the process, you will find that your own troubles become less weighty.

Tough, Flexible, and Optimistic

Dying to self isn't easy. But hard doesn't mean impossible. To take on the challenges of manhood, a man must learn to be tough, flexible, and optimistic. He must be willing to cheerfully carry out his duties, no matter how difficult the situation.

In our family this question has attained the status of a motto: "Are you being tough, flexible, and optimistic?" My boys probably hear that question more often than they would like. But it's a quick and easy reminder that the mantle of manhood isn't something you put down when you get tired, or when things don't go your way. The Bible commands us to "share in suffering as a good soldier of Christ Jesus. No soldier gets entangled in civilian pursuits, since his aim is to please the one who enlisted him" (2 Timothy 2:3-4).

Soldiers don't get to act on their own will. Most people think that military training is about overcoming the enemy. But for me, the biggest test was learning how to conquer myself—how to suck it up and continue to push forward no matter how hard it got. In combat, I saw cold, hungry, exhausted men push on, even when wounded. Mental toughness and the will to stay in the fight were their most powerful weapons.

Men are called to toughness. The majority of people react with surprise when something bad happens to them. They have somehow come to believe that they deserve to be insulated from tragedy. A man doesn't fear trouble; he prepares for it. Life, with a capital "L" is the prize for toughness.

Men don't expect to travel in a personal fast lane. They know nothing worthwhile comes easily, and they look forward to every chance to use their training to effect change. They don't see blessing as "God gives me everything I want" but as "God is always there when nothing else is left."

When life throws a punch, a man learns to roll with it. This concept is easier to grasp when we look at our lives like a bicycle built for two. Christ takes the front seat—and the handlebars—while I sit in back and pedal for all I'm worth. Wherever we end up then, is by his design. As long as I let him steer, I never have to worry about what's around the next corner.

Optimism isn't living with blinders on. It isn't built on false hope. A man understands pessimism profits no one and that griping about something never makes it better. The more hardship a man is willing to embrace, the more fulfilling his life will become, the more adventure he will have, and the more meaning he will find. We can exude a happy confidence, because we trust our Commander.

Please hear me out. Perishing doesn't mean giving up the role of authority. Men are called to lead their families into holiness. Perishing to provide doesn't mean allowing your wife and kids to have everything they ask for while you slave away to pay for it all. When you choose to be "unreasonable" enough to insist on your family doing the right thing, you are resisting the temptation to avoid confrontation. You are acting assertively even when it would be easier to succumb to their wishes. Sometimes a man must be willing to be unreasonable.

Eject! Eject! Eject?

When a pilot's aircraft is damaged and going down in flames, there's only one thing he can do—get out of there. But my "plane" was carrying everything that was most precious to me—my wife and five children. To eject out and leave them behind would clearly reveal the worst kind of passivity, although thousands of examples exist in our society today of men doing just that. No…I wanted to get out *with* my family, not get away from them. I was determined not to settle for making small tweaks in my life. Killing off the passivity in me would require something more extreme.

What we needed was an adventure.

Chapter Seven
Engage

The only thing necessary for the triumph of evil is for good men to do nothing.

—Edmund Burke

To say I'm adventurous is like saying Sasquatch is hairy. It's redundant because it's such an integral part of the creature also known as Bigfoot. My mother must have lived in a chronic state of low-grade panic when I was a kid. Even as a toddler I constantly disappeared into the boulder-strewn desert hills near our home. My after-school antics included hunting under rocks for snakes and scorpions, climbing sheer rock faces, and jumping off the roof of our house. Perhaps the blessing of my safe, stable home primed my need for excitement.

That love of adventure has followed me into adulthood. Today I visit more than a dozen countries each year, most of them conflict or disaster zones. It's what I was made for.

One thing I've learned: true adventure is never comfortable. Two vital factors define adventure: an element of the unknown and the possibility of getting hurt. The challenge of facing hardship and coming out alive on the other side provides the escape. In the midst of such life-or-death experiences, it's hard to worry about the pressures of everyday existence. After all, who can worry about the bills waiting back home when you might drown before the end of the next rapids or fall hundreds of feet down the face of the cliff you are climbing? Adventures put all of life's other pressures on hold, which allows the chance to step away from them and gain perspective.

And perspective was just what my wife and I needed. So after prayerful thought and discussions, Connie and I made the decision to eject from everyday life—not for good, but long enough to gain the perspective we were looking for.

We decided to move to Panama.

Why we chose Panama is another story, but the decision offered the opportunity to move there for a year under the auspices of doing book research. The bigger reason, though, was to escape from all the urgencies and minutiae waiting to assault me every time I walked into my home office. Connie and I believed it would also be good to show our children how the rest of the world lives and that the whole experience would bring us closer together as a family.

The Plan

But people don't just pack up and leave for a year...do they? With every thought, my fears mounted. What if I lost business? How would we handle the added cost of renting a place in Panama? A hundred "what ifs" jumped into my mind.

I took a deep breath and tried to think of the worst-case scenario. If we got down there and it turned out to be horrible, or if we found we just couldn't afford it, we could always come back home and pick up where we left off. In short, we could recover from any possible fallout of our decision.

One year. Long enough, I hoped, to make some lasting changes in my life. The goal? Rid my life of passivity. I determined for that year not to engage in passive activity of any kind. Instead, I would allocate my time for the things most important to me.

That meant no television at all. Not a huge deal since we didn't watch much anyway. But that was just the start. I determined to get up and do the most important things first every day. I would spend focused time in God's Word—not a mere five minutes over a cup of coffee while I listened to the news. No, a true quiet time of reading and prayer.

Then, I would devote serious quality time to my family. I'd have a leisurely cup of coffee with my wife and then do something meaningful with my kids. After that, I would work on my body for at least thirty minutes every day but Sunday. Only then would I sit down at my desk to work.

The Adventure Begins

The actual move turned out to be easier than what I had anticipated. We sold off a few things we could live without (some cows, a trailer) and held an eBay "garage sale" to raise money for our plane tickets. I left a week earlier than the rest of the family and found a moderately priced home for rent in a working class neighborhood where nobody spoke English. Exactly what we wanted. Connie herded the kids and ten large suitcases onto the six-hour flight to Panama. I awaited their arrival with a just-purchased, used Hyundai SUV with a roof rack.

At first it felt as though I'd come out into fresh air after a long time in a stuffy room. The newness of it all was exhilarating. We decided not to buy much furniture for our brief stay, so we used cardboard boxes for end tables and a folding card table for dining. The kids slept on air mattresses for the entire year.

We had no television or central air conditioning. It was fun, like camping, except for one thing...the nagging thought in the back of my mind telling me that we were going to go bankrupt.

My quiet time helped with that. I found myself swinging in the hammock on our front porch and soaking up the Bible, finding new examples almost every day of men like Joshua who were engaged and powerful, and others like King Saul who let passivity ruin their lives. The sights and sounds of our new neighborhood provided an exotic rhythm in the background, and I found myself lingering, not wanting my quiet time to end.

Connie would sometimes join me on the porch, sipping exquisite Panamanian coffee and watching tropical birds flit among the lush greenery in our front yard. Freed from much of the minutiae that normally plagued us back at home, we were able to really enjoy each other's company in an unhurried environment.

The kids and I regularly loaded up in the Hyundai to go exploring. We discovered incredible waterfalls in the jungle, climbed around fifteenth century pirate forts, and watched gigantic ocean-going freighters

transit the Panama Canal. After completing their home schooling each day, the kids ran the neighborhood with the local children, none of whom spoke any English. Because of this immersion in the culture, our kids were speaking Spanish with an astounding level of fluency within four months. The lack of television yielded noticeable benefits: more harmony among our kids, more creative play, and leaner and fitter bodies.

After a few weeks Connie and I found a personal trainer who owned a gym in our area. We signed up, and our thrice-weekly trip to the gym became kind of like a date.

Everything wasn't perfect. In fact, assimilating into a new culture brought with it some very difficult days when we just wanted to crawl into bed, pull the covers over our heads and say, "Call me when the year is over." But these challenges brought us closer as a family.

And Then Came Work

After doing all the important things, I found I had about four hours a day to get my work accomplished. Contrast that to pre-Panama, when I spent close to seventy hours each week behind the computer. I figured the work would never get done, and I'd be losing contracts and eating feathers before the year ended.

Then I began to notice something peculiar. I was getting more done in twenty hours per week than I had been in seventy hours back at home. That difference turned on the proverbial light bulb for me.

Just as a gas expands to fill whatever space it occupies, work expands to fill the time allotted for it. Back at home when I faced an unending stream of work, I would chip away at the mountain until something forced me to quit—usually mealtime, bedtime, or an overworked wife—and not always in that order.

Doing the important things first meant I had to work with an urgency I hadn't felt before. I knew after the first week that I would have to increase my efficiency, or I would never complete my work.

Time for another brutal self-assessment. I tracked the time I spent at work on a minute-by-minute basis and what I found horrified me. I spent several hours each day reading, writing, and shuffling e-mail. In fact, the discoveries of the first few days even embarrassed me, as I found I was checking e-mail literally hundreds of times throughout the day. Obviously, there was no time for that anymore.

I applied to my e-mail a version of the process espoused by Tim Ferris in his bestselling book, *The 4-Hour Workweek*:

1. Eliminate – get rid of as many recurring e-mails as possible
2. Automate – find a way to respond to any e-mails automatically when possible
3. Delegate – filter e-mails through someone else and thereby reduce the clutter in my inbox.[xvi]

Then came the tough part: self-discipline. I stopped leaving my e-mail open on my desktop throughout the day and allowed myself to check and respond only twice per day.

The result? I saved between three and four hours daily. I was stunned!

I then proceeded to apply the above process to every part of my life—paring down the useless minutiae and focusing on the twenty percent of effort that produced eighty percent of the outcome.

The result? Life-changing. In the year we spent in Panama, I wrote two entire books and started a third, grew my income, and did it all on about twenty hours a week in the office. The rest of my time was spent reading, exploring, and reestablishing the relationships that meant the most to me. At the end of the year, I was in better shape than I'd been in twenty years and felt ten years younger because of the lower stress level.

The real test, however, would come when we returned home. Could we maintain our new lifestyle back at our farm in West Virginia, where the little urgencies were waiting to pounce?

The day we left Panama was bittersweet. We had missed our friends and family in America but now had a whole new group of close friends in Panama. After the long flight home, we arrived at the farm in West Virginia and the moment we walked through the door of our log cabin, everyone's response was the same: "We have so much stuff!"

That's when the light went on: A big part of the lower stress level in Panama was due to the fact that we had so little while we were there. Less stuff equals less to worry about. I recalled reading in Randy Alcorn's book *Money, Possessions and Eternity* that the things I own, in reality own me.[xvii] Now I understood clearly what that meant.

Part of keeping the feeling we had in Panama, I realized, meant we'd have to pare down the amount of things that "owned me."

Failing to weed the garden of my life is passivity. I need to constantly be looking for ways to simplify and get rid of that which is worthless. That goes for possessions, relationships, activities, everything. Tearing out each weed of passivity by the roots, no matter what the cost, pays big dividends. Colossians 3:5 says it this way:

> Put to death therefore what is earthly in you: sexual immorality, impurity, passion, evil desire, and covetousness, which is idolatry.

Don't ignore passivity—put it to death. To the extent that a man can track down and eliminate passivity in his everyday journey, life will improve.

The Final Step to Manhood

> Passivity is a compulsion or learned tendency to live at half-speed, which ultimately leaves many men feeling their glass is half-empty and thus half-heartedly committed to projects, plans and goals. Passive men are half in and half out of relationships. Passive men are more attached to not having what they think they want or desire, even though they protest loudly this is not so.[xviii]
> —John Lee, author, life coach, and former professor at the University of Texas

Without Execution, Nothing

"Stand in the door!"

Wind howled through the back of the C-130 cargo airplane as it lumbered through the sky eleven hundred feet above Fryar Drop Zone. The rolling hills of Fort Benning would have been visible out the jump door if I had cared to look, but this being my first jump, I was a little preoccupied.

My fellow classmates at airborne school were lined up behind me in single file, each gripping a static line connected to a cable above our heads. The yellow tubular nylon lines wound through a byte in each man's hand, then around to the rear of his parachute packed in a green nylon tray on his back.

I sure hope these things work like they are supposed to.

Three weeks of arduous training had brought us to this moment. All of the early morning PT runs, the sawdust-covered practice landing falls, the hours of classroom instruction, pushups administered by always-grumpy "black hat" instructors...now everything came down to one step. One really scary 1,100-foot step into the yawning nothingness beyond the door.

If I failed to take this one step, I would never become a paratrooper. Even though I had passed all the classroom exams, perfected the emergency drills, and even suited up and boarded the airplane...none of that mattered if I did not—right now—put that knowledge into action.

The light turned green. The jumpmaster slapped my helmet and shouted, "Go!" I took a deep breath, shut my eyes (practicing for night jumps, you see), and walked out the door.

One step and I was *airborne*. Without that step, I would have been a failure. It wasn't the possession of airborne knowledge that made me qualified—it was the execution.

The Blight of Passivity

Male passivity has moved beyond epidemic proportions across the western world. It has now progressed to the point where it is endemic to the culture. According to a recent study in the United Kingdom, the average man spends *eleven years* of his life in front of the television. Rather than living an adventurous life, he watches make-believe heroes run for a score or make-believe men whose make-believe lives are a caricature of the deep passivity embedded in our culture.

The U.S. Center for Disease Control (CDC) now classifies American culture as "obesogenic." That is, the culture itself is so steeped in unhealthy meal choices, passive activity, and self-indulgence that people in America can't help but get fat. Yet the issue goes much more deeply. Male passivity signifies a part of American culture today just like bloated government.

In fact, one could make a strong case that even bloated government denotes passivity on the part of the voting public.

The Concept of Headship

The very first command God gave to Adam in the Garden of Eden went like this (emphasis mine): "And God blessed them. And God said to them, "*Be fruitful* and multiply and fill the earth *and subdue it*..." (Genesis 1:28).

To subdue something doesn't mean to destroy it—quite the opposite, in fact. It means to conquer something with the aim of making it useful. To bring it under control with the aim of making it better.

God designed a very particular order to the world. When speaking of the Holy Trinity, the order is always Father, Son, and Holy Spirit. The three are co-equals, but on earth Christ did the will of the Father, and after Jesus departed, the Holy Spirit was sent to continue his work. The third verse of 1 Corinthians 11 makes the order clear: the head of every man is Christ and the head of Christ is God. This concept of headship is extremely important.

One spring afternoon I caught a man trespassing on my farm, sitting by our pond with a fishing pole in his hand. He hadn't asked for my permission to be there, so I confronted him with that fact in as friendly a manner as I could.

First I introduced myself as the owner of the property then said, "You need permission to be here."

"Oh, I got permission," he claimed.

"You did? From whom, if you don't mind my asking?"

"Oh, from Mr. P down the road. He told me I could come fish up here."

I couldn't help but laugh, even though it wasn't really funny. "That's nice, but since I'm the property owner, maybe you should ask me next time. Tell you what. I'll give you permission to go fish in Mr. P's pond, if you like."

You can't get the authority to fish in my pond from just anybody. You need to ask me. I'm the only one who can give that authority because the pond belongs to me.

The command to subdue the earth is a bestowal of authority; the verse calls it "dominion" from God to man. This authority hinges on the man's submission to the ultimate ownership of the Creator of the world. But once a man accepts the headship of the Creator, he can then claim the mantle of dominion over his part of the world. Submission puts him in the position to subdue.

First, Subdue Thyself

Before a man can subdue the earth, he must first take dominion over himself. Yes, headship starts with your own head. In Proverbs we learn that "the fear of the Lord is the beginning of knowledge" (Proverbs 1:7). There are three parts to a man's being: spirit, mind, and body. When the spirit is submitted to Christ, it is given authority over the mind and the body. If a man refuses to submit his spirit, then he'll be ruled by his intellect, his emotions, or his appetites. Virtually every problem guys encounter originates from mixing up these three elements. This failure in the natural order results in passivity.

When a guy allows anger to control him, he's being passive because his spirit has lost control of his emotions. Everyone around him will be wounded from the shrapnel.

A guy who follows his appetites will make a god of his belly, his eyes, or some other body part. This makes him a leech on society, a liability to the world at large.

Some guys are just too smart for their own good. Their passivity takes the form of intellectualism that subsumes faith but demands more and more analysis to the point of paralyzing passivity.

Proper headship remedies these issues and many more. A man who can conquer himself will find subduing the rest of his world easy. A man cannot lead well without a sense of self-command.

Passivity Is Pathetic

Actual job opening posted on the Web site Craigslist:

Date: 2010-02-07, 12:54AM CST

Hi,

Well, this is weird. But thanks for clicking and reading.

I don't even know what terms to use. Beautician? Stylist? I haven't been cool for 20+ years, so please just let me talk.

I am a white man who is 46 years old. I'm a dad of teenagers. Middle class.

My wife of many years and I are having big fights, and I want to woo her back. Part of the plan is to not look like the 46-year-old slob that I fear she sees.

I'm no bumpkin--but I'm no metrosexual, either. Honestly, I'm clueless as to fashion, looks, etc.

So what I'm hoping to find: someone (in my mind, it's a woman in her 20s who is young enough to be hip and mature enough to understand me) who will spend a day with me making me more attractive to my wife.

If this sounds weird to you, please don't respond. If you find this ridiculous, please move on.

But if you want to help a decent guy who is in love with his wife, please write. She's back in town on Wednesday--I want my hair and skin and clothes and whatever else to look awesome by then.

I will pay $200 for 8 hours of consulting. You would need to listen to me about the things I know she likes (like curls at the back of my hair), and not try to make me look like I'm 20-something, or anything else I'm not. But I'm very open to a fresh perspective. And, of course, you would need to be respectful, and in earnest.

When you get right down to it, we're all just really trying, right? I need some help. I'm no creeper--I'm not trying to meet someone, or whatever--maybe you're not a 30-something woman, maybe you're a 20- or 80-something gay man or whatever--I don't care. I'm just a middle-aged guy who needs some help in looking as best he can (which won't be much) to try to win his wife back. If you can help, please get in touch.

It'll be a challenge: I have braces, and a bald spot! Well, you play the hand you're dealt.

My wife is the love of my life, and I want nothing more than to be the best I can be for her.

Thanks for reading—I hope you can help.

Well, this is awkward.

Here's a poor guy having trouble in his marriage. He wants desperately to fix it. So desperately, in fact, that he's resorting to hiring *another woman* (or possibly a gay man) to help him update his look.

You've got to give the guy an "E" for effort, I guess. He gets points for realizing that there's something about him that needs to change. More points for wanting to win his wife back. But I daresay it's more than his braces and bald spot that is causing the "big fights" between them.

I believe if we could observe this fellow for an evening in his home, the true problem would soon become clear. A massive point of passivity—or more than one—has most likely infiltrated his family, causing resentment from his wife. I'd guess this guy has never even heard of the concept of headship.

If nothing else, this guy hasn't learned much about women after being married to one for presumably twenty years. Can you imagine their conversation when his wife returns?

Wife: "What happened to you? A new outfit, new shoes and…did you get a manicure?"

Guy: "Sure did. What do you think?"

Wife: "I want to know who bought you those clothes. You don't have the fashion sense to buy anything made by Tommy Bahama…and did you really get a manicure?"

Guy: "Well, see, I hired this college girl and…."

Wife: "You *what?*"

Mayday, Mayday…we're going down…

.

Passive or Passionate?

Looks don't matter to women as they do to men. If they did, the human species would likely not survive. Oh, all other things being equal, a girl prefers a guy who looks like he gives a rip to a mop-headed lump on the couch, but mostly because of what *else* that tells her about the man. What a woman wants is a man who knows how to engage in their relationship and in life. Not passive, but passionate—especially about her.

She wants a man who does things every day to show her that she comes first in his life—before his career, before the kids, before his pastimes—and definitely before any other woman.

I mean, really, if your wife is about to leave you, do you think a goatee or a pair of mantyhose (www.e-mancipate.net) is going to change things? Unfortunately, many relationships disintegrate, because the guy is pursuing things that just don't matter. But he can't even see the glaring areas of passivity causing the real problem.

Passive activity short-circuits your ability to feel the deep emotion needed to be passionate about anything, even the people you love. I'd bet that if Mr. "play the hand you're dealt" unplugged his computer, threw out the television, and sold all his NASCAR memorabilia to put a down payment on that new kitchen his wife has been wishing for, she might believe he was serious about saving the relationship. Better still, if he renounced all forms of passivity and began actually *leading* his family spiritually, rather than just providing for them financially, just think where things could go.

Imagine this scenario:

Hey honey. Can we talk? I just want to apologize for letting our marriage get to this point. I really love you, and I want to change things. So...this might sound strange, but I want to take you and the kids to church this Sunday. Yeah, I know I had that golf thing, but I canceled it. I've decided that I am going to get rid of our cable subscription, too. Let's take the eighty bucks a month from that and have a nice night out together, just you and me. Maybe if we turn off some of the noise around here, we'll be able to get to know each other again. What do you say?

How hard would that be? He's not going to win his family back with a new haircut, and I suspect he knows it, too. He's looking for a relatively inexpensive way to throw some whitewash at the marriage, rather than do the hard work of carrying it to the next level.

That way, if she leaves him for good, he can say it was all her fault. After all, he hired a fashion consultant!

With a little thought most people can figure out what they ought to do. Actually doing it is the tough part. Everyone knows what it takes to be in shape. Exercise regularly and stop eating meat-lover's pizza and deep-fried cheese balls. Lay off the nightly tub of ice cream, and walk a little more than the American-average of 352 steps per day. This isn't rocket science. So if everyone knows what it takes to be healthy, why is obesity becoming a national epidemic?

The answer to that is also simple: a failure to engage. Engaging turns knowing into doing.

In the previous chapters, we've looked at the most important facets of manhood:

- Submit to your Creator and his purpose for your life.
- Honor what is valuable; reject what is worthless
- Assess everything, then improve upon it
- Perish to your desires, and provide for the needs of others.

Implementing each step will turn a boy into a man and will encourage dads who are still figuring it all out. Learning the five steps to manhood will enable an employer to choose wisely when selecting an employee. Knowing these facets of manhood might save a young woman infinite hardship and sadness by helping her discern the best choice for her husband.

After hearing ghastly horror stories about women and the passive guys they choose, I believe it's absolutely vital to teach young women what a man looks like.

The Final Test: Engage

The difference between success and failure in life often comes down to execution — that is, doing what must be done to succeed. You can read every book ever written about investing, but it will never make you wealthy until you put aside the first dollar, then the second, until you have enough capital to work with. And a guy can't truly become a man until he does what's necessary to qualify. Because knowing without doing is worthless.

That's why engagement is the final and truest test of manhood, the capstone in the structure we've been building throughout this book. The first four steps serve as your instructions. I've given you the blueprint and drawn out the plans to construct your monument of manhood. Now it's time to start pounding the nails.

There's no time like the present. I asked my friend Randy Alcorn if he thought passivity is a problem in the church. Here's an excerpt from the e-mail he sent in reply:

There are few greater threats to the church's future than the predominance of passive men. Everywhere I look I see husbands who fail to lead their wives and children in spiritual growth. They spend their time on lawns and boats and golf and television and talk radio, rather than on the study of God's Word and great books centered on Christ and biblical truths.

They talk about current events and sports and work, but not about Jesus. They fail to engage their children on a spiritual level. When their kids hang out with friends that will likely destroy them, they shrug their shoulders and say, "What can you do?" (Try being a man and a dad, interfering with patterns of self-destruction—from Internet pornography to bad friendships, video game, and television addictions—and leading by providing healthy, life-giving alternatives, including good friends and good books.)

Passive dads let their daughters dress in ways that sexually attract young men, and they lack the courage to confront their daughters and wives and draw lines and say, "God has called me to lead this family, and even though you may not realize it, it's harmful to you and dishonoring to Christ to dress that way. I will be held accountable to God if I fail to protect you, whether you (both daughter and wife) like it or not." Active parenting takes time, but in the long run passive parenting takes more time (including meetings with school authorities and police).

Countless Christian dads are irrelevant, so spineless that their wives are left alone to lead the children. These men refuse to take control of the television, Internet, cell phones, kids activities and friends and church attendance and everything else. Instead of being active, leading by example and taking the initiative to be a servant-leader to the glory of God, he passively waits for life to happen, shaking his head in helpless dismay at how poorly things seem to be going. He acts as if there's nothing he can do, as if his family were like the weather, beyond his influence, when in fact God has put him in the position to cultivate spiritual appetites and disciplines. Men are to take the initiative to anticipate and prevent problems and bring solutions to them, not to stand by like cowardly wimps and watch their families be devoured by the Enemy.

A Living Faith

We've talked a lot about passivity throughout this book. The reason is passivity lies at the root of almost everything that keeps guys from becoming the men that God calls them to be. The good news is that, with practice, every man can exercise his God-given authority by hunting down passivity and killing it wherever it lives.

The apostle James put it this way:

What good is it, my brothers, if someone says he has faith but does not have works? Can that faith save him? If a brother or sister is poorly clothed and lacking in daily food, and one of you says to them, "Go in peace, be warmed and filled," without giving them the things needed for the body, what good is that? So also faith by itself, if it does not have works, is dead.

—James 2:14-17

Whenever I find myself wondering if I've really made it as a man, I have only to apply James's questions to the four facets of manhood and ask them of myself.

- Have I submitted my life to God? Am I submitting to the authority he's placed over me? What areas of my life are in rebellion to his will?

- Am I giving my most valuable resources, my time and attention, to the most valuable things in my life?
- Have I taken stock of my life lately? What things can I improve on today?
- How am I consistently putting others' needs ahead of my own? Is there any area in my life where I am acting selfishly?

Reflecting on those questions has become a daily habit during my morning quiet time with life-changing results. My wife sees the difference, too. Here is an excerpt from a very nice note she sent me recently.

Your study of manhood has made such a difference in our marriage. Do you even realize it? As I look around at other marriages, I see so few women who are as secure, loved, protected, and cherished as I feel now.

I especially appreciate how you have chosen to honor the children and me. It is precious to me that you choose to spend time with each child on a regular basis, that you plan trips with them and carve out time at home to invest in the children. Our time with them is so short and you are making the best of that. What a way to honor them!

You have become such a servant to me. I love that you bring me coffee in bed every morning. What a treat! I'm so grateful that you listen and respond when I present you with a "honey do" list and take care of things. When you do that I feel like I am important to you; your time is so limited and that makes me feel even more special when you take time to do the things that I ask of you.

It fills me up with love for you when I see you pour into our children. You instruct them, love on them, and listen to them. They adore you for that. You are such an involved daddy. Better than I even imagined that you would be.

I have thanked God many times that he has laid the subject of manhood on your heart. I'm thankful that you take it so seriously. What a change it has made in our marriage and the children and their future. I'm excited to see the men that you will raise out of our boys and the men that the girls will chose under your guidance. I have great hope for the success of our family because of all the effort you put into becoming a better and better man of God.

Take No Prisoners

Why be comfortable with "good enough" when we were made for so much more? Without a doubt, just existing is more comfortable than adventurous living. But that's not what men were made for.

Each man has points of passivity, areas where he chooses inaction over action, whether he knows it or not. Some are easier than others to spot, but a man must abhor them all. Whenever I have the opportunity to speak to men, I always try to admonish them: don't simply shun passivity; hunt it down and choke the life out of it, or it will multiply until it consumes you.

Every guy's weaknesses will be different, and many will involve things that might be considered good on their own. Take work, for example. Men were made to work. It is our duty. But without proper balance, it can easily consume things that are even more important.

Passivity doesn't always come in the form of inaction. Being too busy is a very common point of passivity, one that I struggle with constantly. I must regularly weed the garden of my time. Doing more doesn't always mean accomplishing more. Men often fill their schedules with meaningless activities to feel and look important.

Sometimes that comes at the expense of harder tasks more central to their character as a man, like having a conversation with a dissatisfied wife or spending time with a friend who is hurting.

A lot of angry, demanding husbands might miss the fact that their passivity is manifested in their failure to control their emotions and maintain a home environment where everyone feels loved and protected.

Rules of Engagement

Engaging as a man requires a combat mentality. We have to see time wasters as enemies trying to blow up bridges and impede our progress as we try to advance the kingdom of God. In combat, comfortable will get you killed. Embracing hardship is central to godly manhood.

Passion can easily get buried beneath a mountain of passive activity. In the first chapter of second Timothy, Paul commanded his protégé to "fan into flame the gift of God, which is in you through the laying on of my hands" (2 Timothy 1:6).

This is what a man does. To find the work he was made to do, he must "fan into flame" the passion that's within him. That can't happen when he's engaged in passive activity.

Many young men I speak to have no idea what I'm talking about. When I ask, "What fires you up?" too often the answer is, "Uh…I dunno."

God has placed an ember in every man, a spark to set off a purpose that moves him to action. A man's job is to find that passion and uncover it within himself, then coax it, feed it, and follow it. Passive activity smothers the flame like dirt. Spending one's time in constructive pursuits uncovers a man's gifts and sets him on a course to fulfill his purpose. Psalm 34 tells us that whoever loves life must *flee* from evil and *seek* peace and *pursue* it (Psalm 34: 12-14). Notice the action words. Manhood is not a spectator sport. You've got to get in the game.

A Commission

Cutting all the weeds out makes the garden grow, but the weeds will be back. That's why this must become a daily process, like brushing one's teeth. Jesus told his disciples that if they loved him, they would do what he told them. Yes, they had to know his commands, but their knowledge was incomplete without obedience.

Engagement is the sum total of putting into practice the first four principles outlined in this book. The call extends to every nook and cranny of our lives.

Socially, a man must be a relentless force for good, shining so brightly that those who dwell in darkness can barely stand the sight of him. Spiritually, a man must lead his household as if he is the pastor and they are his church. Relationally, he must always strive to be the catalyst for improvement, creating a harmonious environment free of the poison of gossip, harsh words, and bitterness. Physically and emotionally, a man makes sure to do hard things regularly, lest his body and spirit grow soft and flabby, unfit for the tasks ahead.

Graduation

After my son Mason and I completed this study, we took a five-night canoe trip to celebrate his twelfth birthday. We invited some of his friends along, as well as their fathers and another of my son's mentors, my brother-in-law, Cory. Each night around the campfire Mason explained one of the five tenets of manhood from this study to his peers, while I gave input along the way.

On the last night we held a small ceremony. Now that Mason had demonstrated his understanding of the subject matter, we men took turns encouraging him, pouring out affirmations of his character and potential and making known our expectations for him as he works to develop these precepts of manhood. Then, we welcomed him into the brotherhood of men by presenting to him a KA-BAR knife, engraved with his name and 1 Peter 1:13, one of the verses we studied together: "Therefore, preparing your minds for action, and being sober-minded, set your hope fully on the grace that will be brought to you at the revelation of Jesus Christ."

I told him, "Mason, manhood is like a razor-sharp KA-BAR knife. Used properly, it can build, protect, and provide. But wielded carelessly, it can bring untold hurt and destruction. Let this knife remind you of the responsibility you now bear."

Cory then presented Mason with a Bible, and we talked about how it was similar to a compass. "A compass will help you get where you want to go," Cory said, "but only if you use it. The Bible is relevant to every tough decision you will ever have to make. It will guide you, protect you, encourage and convict you. It will help you mature into full, godly manhood. But it doesn't work unless you pick it up and use it— just like a compass."

As our small ceremony concluded around the campfire, I thought back on the different manhood rituals I'd read about. I imagined the Hebrew boy of Jesus' day reading from the Torah before the congregation, then being welcomed into the fellowship of men. I thought about the Spartan boys of the *agoge,* being constantly reminded that the hardships they were made to endure were to steel them for the day of battle. I saw another campfire, nearly thirty years ago, where godly men took the time to tell me—and show me—what manhood looked like.

And then I thought of Jesus, the ultimate man.

Jesus, the Manliest of All Men

Jesus was the one man who got it all right. The One who came to earth precisely to show us what fully formed manhood ought to look like. In him are found all five facets discussed in this book. In fact, the more anyone reads about Jesus of Nazareth, the bolder and starker these principles become.

1. **Submit:** Jesus was fully submitted to the Father. Not just when it was easy, either. Recall the prayer in the garden of Gethsemane the night Jesus was arrested and taken away to be crucified: "Father, if you are willing, remove this cup from me. Nevertheless, not my will, but yours, be done" (Luke 22:42). This short verse shows how Jesus, fully God, yet fully man, overcame the temptation to take the easy way out so that the rest of us could escape the penalty of our own sin. What an awesome, mind-bending thing to think about!

2. **Honor:** Jesus demonstrated value in a way that shows us how we should live in this world. He

healed on the Sabbath, made time for the children, and elevated the status of women everywhere. He worked diligently but knew when to take a rest. He feared nothing, because he knew everything was a part of God's plan.

3. **Assess and Improve:** Jesus said it himself: "For the son of man came to seek and to save the lost" (Luke 19:10). His entire existence on earth was about fixing a broken world, redeeming the human race, and making people's lives better. He healed the sick, performed miracles, and even provided new wine when the drinks ran out at a wedding. In big ways and small, Jesus saw what needed to be fixed and set about making things right. That's what a man does.

4. **Perish and Provide:** The cross on Calvary says it all. Jesus died in our place to provide heaven for those who will accept it.

5. **Engage:** Never a spectator, Jesus was engaged in every area of life, even, so, *especially* when it required difficult confrontations and expensive choices. Jesus did the right thing no matter what. Comfort was very low on his list, because he was on a mission.

As he was, so we should be.

Jesus was and is the total package. In any area of life, the more a man can learn to emulate him, the better he and his world will become. Following Jesus and his example won't be easy, comfortable, or safe. Then again, who needs those things?

Men are made for adventure.

Recommended Resources for Making Men

The ALERT Academy
www.alertacademy.com

The sprawling 2600-acre campus just outside Big Sandy, Texas, is a hive of activity, even in the early summer heat of West Texas. A team of men in crisp blue uniforms rappels from a 110-foot tower while a fire truck rolls by with siren screaming. Another group is clustered around an instructor, learning how to administer CPR to a plastic dummy on the ground.

It's a typical day at the International ALERT Academy, a course for young men that turns boys into men in just under one year's time. It's kind of a cross between a monastic order and the Green Berets. The men spend their time at the academy without the comforts of music, movies or girls—probably the three most important things to most guys their age—and they do it out of necessity.

In order to become trained at skills like diving, flying, disaster relief, emergency medicine, construction, plumbing, electrical, auto maintenance, firefighting, land navigation, and wilderness survival, just to name a few, they can't afford distractions.

In addition, each class learns to recite entire books of the Bible and deploys around the world on missions of disaster relief, humanitarian aid, and missionary aid and security. Upon completion of the program, the men are qualified to enter the workforce as first responders, but many of them choose the mission field or the military.

Colonel John Tanner, who leads the academy, likes to point out that most teen guys graduate high school without a clue. They can play *Halo* and surf Facebook like pros, but put a chainsaw in their hands and somebody's in for a trip to the hospital.

A hundred years ago most teen boys could work with their hands and had at least a modicum of practical skill in building and fixing things. Today, most boys wouldn't know the difference between a hack saw and a table saw. More importantly, they are woefully undereducated in things that matter for eternity.

The ALERT Academy has been fixing that problem, making men out of momma's boys since 1994. Highly recommended for your young men.

The Timothy Group
www.timothygroup.org

Led by former Air force Major (ret) Bruce Stansbury, the Timothy group runs a high-octane adventure camp for young men each fall. The camp uses survival training, rappelling, firearms training and more to give young men the challenge of their lives, presenting seemingly-insurmountable objectives in a high-stress leadership-building environment. Every step includes full-tilt training in Godly manhood and the characteristics of servanthood required to develop leaders of men.

The Master's Mission

www.mastersmission.org

Most of today's full-time missionaries come from middle-class suburban America. As such, those who commit themselves to service abroad rarely come with the skills necessary to survive and thrive in the developing world. The Master's Mission exists to privide them with these skills, and in an intensive eleven-month course, trains missionary families on such things as alternative power generation, construction techniques, auto maintenance, developing clean water supplies, self-protection skills, farming and animal husbandry and homeschooling, along with a comprehensive Bible curriculum. For men who want to gain the skills necessary to provide for their families while serving on themission field, the training offered by the Master's Mission is second to none.

Recommended Reading:

- *The Death of the Grown Up*-by Diana West
- *Margin: Restoring Emotional, Physical, Financial, and Time Reserves to Overloaded Lives*-by Richard Swensen
- *Don't Waste Your Life*-by John Piper
- *Future Men*-by Douglas Wilson
- *Boyhood and Beyond*-by Bob Schultz
- *Ordering Your Private World*-by Gordon McDonald
- *Courageous: a Novel*-by Randy Alcorn
- *Raising a Modern-Day Knight: A Father's Role in Guiding His Son to Authentic Manhood*-by Robert Lewis

Other Books by Chuck Holton:
(www.livefire.us)
- A More Elite Soldier – Pursuing a Life of Purpose
- Bulletproof – The Making of an Invincible Mind
- Stories from a Soldier's Heart (with Alice Gray)
- The Task force Valor Novel Series
    1. Allah's Fire
    2. Island Inferno
    3. Meltdown

Acknowledgements

One of the benefits of traveling around the country speaking to men's groups is that I get to meet lots of men who share my passion for true manhood and raising boys into it. Over the last ten year's I've developed an amazing network of friends, men who challenge me, mentor me, encourage me and hold me accountable. This book would never have come to be without them.

One of those men is my friend Trevor Williams, a reporter for Global Atlanta and fully devoted fellow soldier in God's army. Trevor labored over my scattered notes, speeches and blog postings to build the structure that got this project off the ground. For his help I am deeply grateful.

Mike McFarland could have written this book himself. Another of the circle of friends I've found in my travels, Mike is the father of seven and one of the few men I've met who takes the job of raising Godly sons and daughters more seriously than I do.

Mike is a great inspiration to me and to his own sons, whose maturity reflects his commitment to them. Mike and his son Josiah are the subjects of the photo on the cover of this book, which I snapped on a backpacking trip a few years ago.

My faithful editor, Judy Gordon, has worked tirelessly on several of my books, and is responsible for getting me my first book contract back in 2002. Her prayers helped with this project at least as much as her editiing expertise. Janet McHenry's amazing skill as a type editor helped make this project actually begin to look like a book. If you find any flaws in the manuscript, you'll have found a place where I probably added something last-minute after she'd finished her checking. So blame me, not her.

Last, I'd like to say thanks to the men who invested in me to teach me what manhood is all about, starting with my own father, Mike Holton. I have only to look around at the majority of families in this country today to see what an incredible difference a devoted dad can make. My life is no exception. There were many others, though. Men like Ken Strunk, Ken Inzer, David Randal, Mike Hare, Chuck Hull, and Oliver North.

May your efforts be compounded in me through this work, and may God reward you for your faithfulness in making men.

About the Author

Chuck Holton is a bestselling author, war correspondent and disaster reporter, photographer, documentary video producer, public speaker, adventurer, businessman, husband and father of five children.

After serving four years in the U.S. Army with the Elite 75th Ranger Regiment and four flying helicopters as an Aeroscout Observer in the National Guard, Chuck went on to a successful career as a stockbroker. Ten years later, he began to feel compelled to spend more time with his family, so he left Wall Street behind to become a full-time writer.

Chuck is now the author of seven books including Bulletproof, A More Elite Soldier, Stories from a Soldier's Heart and the Task Force Valor Series. He also collaborates with LtCol Oliver North (USMC Retired) on the new York Times bestselling American Heroes series of books.

As a backpack journalist and freelance video producer, Chuck travels to more than a dozen hot spots around the globe each year.

In the past several years, he has trekked across unexplored jungle islands, traveled into Burma with the Karen Rebel Army, embedded with U.S. Troops in Iraq, Afghanistan and the Horn of Africa, reported from Congo, Northern Ireland, Central and South America, Lebanon, Eastern Europe, Mexico and more. His varied interests include backpacking, scuba diving, farming, exploring, and studying world religions.

Chuck's video dispatches are often featured on the Christian Broadcasting Network, where he also maintains the blog Boots on the Ground. He frequently speaks to churches and other organizations around the world on the topics of Biblical manhood, life structuring, adoption, homeschooling and other charitable and patriotic causes. Chuck's idea of a vacation is a week of uninterrupted time at his farm in Appalachia with Connie and their five children.

Chuck accepts a limited number of speaking engagements each year. To make a request, please contact Dana Ashley at Ambassador Speaker's Bureau at 615-370-4700.

We'd love to hear your feedback about this book. To contact Chuck directly, find him on facebook at www.facebook.com/chuckholton/ or email makingmenbook@gmail.com

[i]*Endnotes*
Diane West, The Death of the Grown-Up: How America's Arrested Development Is Bringing Down Western Civilization (New York: St. Martin's Press, 2007).

[ii] Grace and Fred M. Hechinger, Teen-Age Tyranny (Robbinsdale, Minn.: Fawcett Publications, 1963).

[iii] Holman Christian Standard Bible (Nashville, Tenn.: B&H Publishing Group, 2011).

[iv] Ibid.

[v] Steven Pressfield, The Warrior Ethos (New York: Black Irish Entertainment, LLC, 2011).

[vi] Douglas Wilson, Future Men (Moscow, Id.: Canon Press, 2001).

[vii] Lucius Annaeus Seneca, On the Shortness of Life (New York: Penguin Press, 2005).

[viii] Associated Press, "What Price Vanity? #14 Million for License Plate," MSNBC.com, February 18, 2008, http://www.msnbc.msn.com/id/23218590/ns/world_news-weird_news/t/what-price-vanity-million-license-plate/#.TmwyCa7X_B8.

[ix] "The Most Expensive Number Plates in the World…Ever!" Demon Plates, September 10, 2011, http://www.demonplates.com/plates/expensive-number-plates.php.

[x] John Piper, Don't Waste Your Life (Wheaton, Ill.: Crossway, 2003).

[xi] Randy Alcorn, "Two Sources of Self-Esteem: Secular and Christian," Eternal Perspective Ministries, February 16, 2010, http://www.epm.org/resources/2010/Feb/16/two-sources-self-esteem-secular-christian/.

[xii] Chuck Holton, "Becoming a Family Man," Focus on the Family, December 2003, http://www.focusonthe

family.com/parenting/parenting_roles/the_un involved_
      father/family_man.aspx.

[xiii] "Ranger Creed," United States Army, September 10, 2011, http://www.army.mil/values/ranger.html.

[xiv] Chuck Holton, "The Heart of a Ranger," CBN Online, August 10, 2009, http://blogs.cbn.com/bootson
      theground/archive/2009/08/10/the-heart-of-a-ranger.aspx.

[xv] "The Measure of a Man," Homesteading Today, December 29, 2008, http://www.homesteadingtoday.
      com/archive/index.php/t-285996.html.

[xvi] Tim Ferris, The 4-Hour Workweek (New York: Crown Archetype, 2009).

[xvii] Randy Alcorn, Money, Possessions, and Eternity (Carol Stream, Ill.: Tyndale House Publishers, 2003).

[xviii] John Lee, "The Half-Lived Life: Why Overcoming Passivity Is So Important," Positive Health Online, March 2011, http://www.positivehealth.com/article/personal-growth/the-half-lived-life-why-overcoming-passivity-is-so-important

Made in the USA
San Bernardino, CA
08 January 2013